1. Dream Girl Dreaming, 1960, brush and ink, 16⅞ x 14, Abe Lerner, New York.

THE GRAPHIC WORK OF
Philip Evergood

SELECTED DRAWINGS AND COMPLETE PRINTS

By Lucy R. Lippard

FOREWORD BY ABRAM LERNER

PROEM BY JAMES A. MICHENER

CROWN PUBLISHERS, INC., NEW YORK

© 1966 BY THE ART DIGEST, INC.

LIBRARY OF CONGRESS CATALOG CARD NUMBER: 65-17022

DESIGNED BY ABE LERNER

PRINTED IN THE U.S.A. BY THE MERIDEN GRAVURE COMPANY

e. 1

Contents

2. Juju and Her Dog, 1961, brush and ink, 37 x 24, Selden Rodman, Oakland, N. J.

Foreword

ONE ALWAYS seems to begin with the fact that Philip Evergood is a "social artist," if only because Evergood has repeated it so often. What the term means exactly is hard to define; its origins go back to other generations, other times. Briefly, it probably means involvement in the social scene, awareness of the human condition, and a willingness to make one's art a weapon in effecting social change or reform. In any case, it is an esthetic commitment not likely to be discussed in today's art circles.

This is undoubtedly a reaction to the Thirties and Forties when social art, like regional art before it, had a considerable following among artists and public. Those of us old enough to remember the mood of that day, the era of the unmitigated Depression, will recall that it was more hospitable to ideas of social change than the decades following the Second World War. Many artists, sensitive to these social currents and inspired by the revolutionary art of the Mexican muralists, sought confirmation and revelation in the graphic essays of Goya and Daumier, the peasant paintings of the Le Nains, the unadorned themes of Chardin and, closer to their own time, the tragic vision of Van Gogh and Soutine. These artists and numerous others demonstrated the variety of attitudes and styles that could be labelled "social art." Social involvement and social theme seemed to offer them a way out of the parochialism of formalist art, which they held to be historically passé and incapable of dealing with the dramatic changes in American life. They also believed they were continuing the native realist tradition of Homer, Eakins, and the Ashcan School.

I must confess that I have never been keen on labelling Philip's art. He is obviously so protean in his conceptions, in fact so non-conformist, there is no reason why his work should be classified with that of rhetoricians, table-pounders, or political cartoonists.

What distinguishes Evergood is his gift for blending plastic invention with an unusual treatment of theme. He has always been alert to the formal developments of the 20th century, as the drawings in this book will testify. He has experimented widely with those components which finally determine the pictorial quality of a work of art, insisting only that the figurative elements remain as the basic psychological structure.

The metaphors he paints brim with bizarre imagery and invention that transcend the everyday themes which inspire them. They soar off into a world of fantasy and humor (constant elements in his art) which challenge reason and order; they transform men and women into heroes and satyrs, earth-mothers and sirens, factories into Gothic fancies, and evil exploiters into Ensor-like buffoons.

Miss Lippard points out in this book how the drawings and prints relate to the paintings, how they serve as an archive of ideas for reflection and reference. Evergood is the first to insist that he is not a professional print maker, that he is not interested in experimenting with new techniques or in widening the horizons of printmaking. His etchings and drawings are created out of the same compulsion as his paintings, to shape his fantasies into a vital and communicable form. He tries a new medium much as a batter tries a new bat, the better to hit the ball.

Aside from the differences in technique and media, what gives drawing its special character is the artist's intention. Before the 16th century most artists considered their drawings as preparatory studies for paintings. Their notebooks were filled with ideas for future works, detailed studies for works in progress, schematic solutions for problems of scale and pictorial space. Shortly after the beginning of the 16th century artists began to see in drawing the possibilities of full and definitive esthetic expression.

The contemporary artist uses drawing as a

completely independent and legitimate art form, only stylistically related to his paintings. We value drawings for the way they disclose the artist's most subtle inner vision. The medium's limitations impose themselves constanly and demand an economy and virtuosity which never fail to interest us. We "read" a drawing even before we feel or grasp its total meaning.

Evergood's drawings and prints admit us to an inner world of experience and reflection. They are inventions by a man of fierce resolution, high spirits, and great tenderness. They are about people whose lives have touched his heart, about miners and railroad workers, Saturday's children, good friends, New York, visions from the Old Testament, the artist as hero and jester. These are extraordinary drawings, full of that bounce and exuberance I always identify with Evergood's art.

It is a happy occasion for me to see them assembled so handsomely here and to observe that they are as fascinating today as when I first encountered them almost thirty years ago.

ABRAM LERNER
Curator Joseph H. Hirshhorn Collection

Proem: An Opinion

FOR ME to offer a few words in conjunction with this presentation of Philip Evergood's work is to repay a debt of more than thirty years standing.

It was in the depression that I first became aware of the powerful painting, imagery and intellectual content of the work that Evergood was doing. His pictures struck me with great force because they depicted a society that I, myself, was experiencing and they depicted it with truth and insight.

Through the years I followed the work of this strong painter. Whenever I had a chance I saw his paintings in exhibitions, I also had a chance to visit in different cities his retrospective shows, and I became familiar with almost all that he had done. The more I saw, the more pleased I was.

Some years ago, it became a real pleasure for my wife and me to acquire one of the very finest of the Evergood canvases, the depiction of the famous marathon dances which were such a blight on our society some decades ago. In his canvas Evergood caught the whole sordid story in a way that not even any writer, with the possible exception of Horace McCoy's, *They Shoot Horses Don't They,* was able to do. Today that picture remains as fresh and real as when I first saw it, and is one of my favorites.

In recent years the paintings which my wife and I have collected have tended toward the nonobjective because so much fascinating work was being done in that genre, but even though our sympathies often lay with that school of painting, we never lost our interest in the representational school, so that it was social paintings by Sloan, Benton, Gropper and Philip Evergood which held a large share of our interest. I think that any society which produced an art form which was not offering criticism and review would be a defunct society, and its art form would be serving very poorly indeed.

It is for these reasons that I am honored to participate in a presentation of Evergood's work.

JAMES A. MICHENER

[8]

3. Woman with Dog, 1961, brush and ink, watercolor, 36½ x 23½, Dr. and Mrs. Arthur E. Kahn, New York.

4. Studies for "Mine Disaster", (c.1933), pencil, 13⅜ x 11, the artist.

The Graphic Work of Philip Evergood

I. INTRODUCTION

IT IS NEVER EASY to separate one part of a man's life-work from the rest, and any study of Philip Evergood's art—his graphics as well as his painting—has less to do with questions of style than with the man himself. Both evade generalization. Evergood is a man of contrasts—an emotional and artistic spendthrift. His personality, his subjects, and his methods contrast and often collide, as though the artist were deliberately foiling anyone who would attempt to categorize him. Herman Baron—the man most responsible for encouraging and developing Evergood as an artist—compared him to Whitman. Robert Coates said he was "mad as Poe," while John Baur called him a Gulley Jimson. His faith in spontaneity and his instinctive distrust of the predetermined work of art are responsible for his successes and his failures.

Yet Evergood's great strength is that he is not afraid of failure. Although sensitive to criticism, of which he has had more than his share, he continues to go his own way. In the course of a forty-year career his profound involvement with contemporary life and humanity have often overwhelmed considerations of technique, esthetics, and art for art's sake. His exuberance and honesty have molded the contradictions of his art into a vibrantly recognizable unity. Bold, careless, heartfelt line, thin, precise and tender line, realism and distortion, simplicity and chaos—all are in the end distinctly Evergood. It is very difficult to balance an art continually on the brink of excess, but Evergood is in up to his neck. Interested primarily in extremes, "in an age of masks, he is often and openly himself."[1]

Drawing is by definition an "intimate, subtle, often searchingly personal statement, the pinning down in visual form of an idea or mood which the artist is attempting to define within a pictorial medium, an exacting shorthand which closely charts and symbolizes the ideas and discoveries of the perceptive artist."[2] Thus we can expect to see the creative skeleton of Evergood's entire art emerge in his drawings, more clearly perhaps than in the oils, since a drawing at best retains all the freshness of the original impulse, often lost or transformed in painting. His graphic work has been even more diverse than his painting. Recent drawings show Evergood still pursuing total expressiveness and spontaneity, retaining a quality which might have been imagined accessible only to youth.

The basis of Evergood's drawing technique

is the opposition of different types of line, no matter how variously it may be employed. "I believe that the whole interest of art depends very much on the relationship of sharpness to softness, of disappearing edge to defined edge, on the lack of monotony between the accented moment and the let-go moment. You don't always feel strong enough to do that. I've done drawings that I've looked at afterwards and found banal and monotonous because I hadn't been inspired at the time to know where to accent one sweeping line with another brittle, wiry line. But on the other hand, when I feel that I've been successful, it's always been the little sharp drawing of a toe or finger or an eye-lid in relation to a big kind of smoothness and lost-edge quality."[3]

Evergood's versatility as a draughtsman is an important part of his work as a painter. He consistently uses line, not only for emphasis, but as an essential stylistic element. To finish an oil, he usually draws over it in black paint. This is one reason he is not fashionable in certain circles today, when formal quality alone is emphasized. Picasso is another twentieth-century artist who frequently draws over or around his initially painted forms. Evergood, who is determinedly against art for art's sake, sees nothing wrong with this process. He draws over his pigment literally to underline the sense of the thing, because sense and feeling are as important to him as appearance, and the black contours crystallize both image and intention.

One of the most unusual aspects of Evergood's art is his extraordinary capacity to retain his esthetic innocence through an eventful and complicated life—the details of which have been related elsewhere.[4] This quality has struck some critics as affected or false and it is responsible for some of their most frequent epithets: "overstated," "obvi-

ous," "too explicit," and so on. The fact that over forty years ago Evergood lived in England as a child and attended Eton and Cambridge, both briefly and not too happily, has prejudiced certain observers. "In discussing a 'primitive' and 'folksy' and 'naive' quality in my painting, they are quick to judge me by what they have read about my history. I've been called 'the most sophisticated innocent in the world.' Some have gone so far as to suggest that I am putting on some kind of 'act,' some sort of deception on the innocent public—all because I really *am* simple, direct and natural in my approach to people and to life. My father and mother were the same—we lived that way. And I've continued to retain a certain innocence despite all the vileness and dirtiness I've seen while knocking around this world. I'm very grateful to Providence for my capacity to remain a child even though I've seen a lot and suffered a lot which should make me into a full-grown man."

The development of Evergood's personal brand of "sophisticated innocence" can be followed in his drawings and prints up to 1932, when his art and personality met to form a mature style. But its roots go far back. A portrait of his father (*p. 13*) executed at the age of eleven (1912) is amazingly close to the Evergood we know. Here are the broad, spontaneous line, the fresh vision, the distortion, the direct approach. Superficially, only a few years might separate this from the harsh, assured dislocations of the 1964 *Carpaccio and the Dudas* (fig. *111*). But the latter is based on half a century of learning and then learning to forget. After an extremely strict education in draughtsmanship, Evergood's personal tendency towards an outwardly awkward but deeply felt and powerful expression finally triumphed. The catalyst was the

[12]

heightened social awareness brought on by the Depression years in America.

II. EDUCATION AND EARLY WORK

Evergood's father, Myre Evergood Blashki, a sensitive impressionist landscape painter and friend of Albert Ryder, was proud to say that Philip was "the artist in the family." His mother, Flora Jane Perry, was British, and Philip's childhood was spent as much in England as in America. After tentative advances toward a career in the Navy and then

5. Portrait of Father, (c.1912), pencil, 6¼ x 5⅜, the artist.

in the Law, and a year at Cambridge, he realized that his sole ambition was to become an artist. He had been drawing all his life and had even won a prize at Eton. A pencil portrait of his mother done in 1919, in spite of its uniform and untrained line, is a perceptive likeness which equals the later portraits in eloquence. With the encourage-

ment of a Cambridge Don and the sculptor Havard Thomas, the twenty-year-old Evergood showed his drawings to Henry Tonks of the famous Slade School of Art in London, who assured the young man that he could not draw. "But," he added, "your drawings did something that few do, which is a good thing. They made me laugh."

With his acceptance at Slade, Evergood settled down to learn "how to draw." He was exposed to one of the most rigorous academic art educations available at the time. London was still a backwater and little modern or avant-garde art was seen or discussed. The school's methods were confined to traditional doctrines. Tonks, who had been a surgeon, taught that drawing was "a delicate operation." The point of the pencil was for one thing, the side for another; the model was to be seen through the eyes of the Renaissance man. "The Slade taught beautiful simple methods of the great old masters, but then the tempo and humor of life went beyond it. I thought, I'm a little SOB who's going to cut loose and find my own way, but while I'm here I'll swallow my pride and learn all the little tricks of the masters."

The drawings surviving from the Slade period show that Evergood did indeed learn these tricks. Various studies after antique casts (some of which have Tonks' corrections in the margin) and especially two sketches of a male model dated 1921 (*fig. 17*) show how well he had learned. But while the style is assured, correct and properly conservative, there remains something of the Evergood whose drawings had provoked laughter, the Evergood who was to be, within two decades, one of America's most original artists. The figure at the right, despite its basic anatomical accuracy, suggests Gauguin rather than Raphael. There is a powerful awkwardness, an attraction away from grace toward strength,

[13]

a disregard for "beauty" as such, which were to be keynotes of the vintage Evergood. In many of the other academic studies done at the Slade this quality was completely obscured in favor of lifeless perfection, but Evergood's inclinations were already evident. "I went to the best schools," he was to say later, "and that is where I developed a sense of humor."

A trip to America in 1922 produced several drawn portraits (*figs. 19, 20*), which show the fruits of the Slade regime. Very unlike Evergood's strident mature work, the delicate parallel line technique was especially suited to portrait and genre subjects. This was to be his drawing style for several years. The likenesses already so skilfully traced before were now crystallized with the aid of this accomplished technique. During the twenties, his parents, with their contrasting features and personalities, were among Evergood's favorite portrait subjects. "My father had one of the most beautiful 'Eastern' faces, a strong beak nose and an arab-like quality." The mother was a great influence on Evergood's life. His interpretations of her fine, spiritual countenance are extremely personal, recording her progressive emaciation from cancer, of which she died in 1927, and the son's sensitivity to her suffering. "My mother had had all the advantages of travel and education. She spoke several languages. She was interested in music. A person of great intellect and moral principles, a terrifically courageous person." Several of the portraits of her may be considered studies for the major painting dated 1927/46, in which the artist was seeking a "mystery, a kind of moon-like, out-of-the-world quality."

In 1923, armed with his hard-earned Slade certificate, Evergood returned to New York for a year. "I had an insatiable desire to learn how to draw, despite the two exacting years at Slade. Now I needed to get down to earth."

Besides sketching nights at the Educational Alliance Art School, he studied drawing at the Art Students League with William von Schlegell and George Luks. The former was a sensitive draughtsman who never had a one-man show before his death. "Countless artists studied with him and owed their first knowledge of the moderns to his teaching. Freedom was his watchword. He held the individuality of the student as inviolate."[5] The exuberant Luks may have helped to instill a dissatisfaction with academies and inner-directed art in general. His was a combination of romanticism and red-blooded realism close to that which Evergood himself was to evolve, "the expression of a robust love of life. . . . Humanity was the center of his art; he enjoyed painting the least conventional aspects of life around him, finding something picturesque in the crudest and commonest themes."[6] This might have been written about Evergood himself fifteen years later. It shows that he was in good hands.

The most important event of Evergood's year in New York was his introduction to the technique of etching. In early 1924 he did his first print independently in his Greenwich Village room. It was a drypoint, *Portrait of an Old Jew (fig. 115)*, an attractive but totally academic head rendered in a soft, wispy line. It was followed by his first etching, a fine line portrait of the painter, Philip Reisman (*fig. 116*), who owned a press and was primarily responsible for Evergood's new interest. The 1924-25 sojourn in Paris interrupted further use of the new skills and it was only on Evergood's return to New York in 1926 that he really began to work seriously, and personally, in the intaglio media.

Evergood stayed in Paris only a year, but it was an important one. He exhibited a print at the Salon d'Automne, began to paint in earnest, met his future wife—the ballet dancer

[14]

Julia Cross—and gained a clearer idea of his own artistic directions. At first he studied at the Academie Julian, where he was disgusted with the master's trivial comments and the French students' practical jokes. Then came a brief period spent in André Lhote's courses. "I wanted to draw, but he persuaded me to paint. I didn't like his approach at all. By that time I knew Pascin and was much impressed by his work; this was just the opposite. Lhote was most insensitive to anything new and insisted on black shadows around everything; his approach was a formula. Pascin's work was sensitively fumbled and felt, and that was my own inclination. How am I going to teach myself to paint? I thought. I don't believe in lessons."

At this point he met the British painter, Athelstan Hiddingh, and MacNeil Siple, an American architect and painter. These two, with their discussions and superior knowledge of both technique and art history, filled in the lacunae in Evergood's background. "This came just at the right moment, gave me more knowledge of what art was *about,* the foundation, so I could just go out and *look.* I had abandoned the academies and wasn't considered any good by anyone except those two, who thought I needed discipline of another variety than that taught in schools. 'If you find something to say, you'll be a good painter,' Siple told me." The three young men hired "odd models, blind men and seamstresses," and often worked together. "I decided to start from the ground up, with no preconceived notion of anything. The study of academic drawing at the Slade was now insufficient in today's world."

Three handsome drawings from 1925 show the seeds of this revolt. Evergood says everything from that time was "just doodling," but it was slowly serving to loosen up "muscles" almost incapacitated by an overdose of aca-

6. Hiddingh Painting, (1925), pen and sepia ink, 10⅜ x 8, the artist.

demic disciplines. Two sketches of *Hiddingh Painting (above),* and those of a French girl, Simone, with whom Evergood was in love *(fig. 30),* are expressive, confident and, above all, fluid and free. The tight parallel lines of the earlier portraits had become an expressive calligraphy. In *Job on the Dunghill (fig. 18),* the Cézannesque rendering found in prints and paintings of similar subject matter is transformed into a whirling oval of line. This was done in the South of France, in Cagnes, where Evergood came to rest briefly after

[15]

touring Italy and studying for about six weeks at the British Academy in Rome. Then he returned to New York to be with his mother, whose health was rapidly declining.

The drawings from 1926-29 show a slow evolution from the fluid but still rather academic style of late 1925 into a much freer and more personal expression. Evergood continued to make conventional studies from the model as a discipline to keep his hand in. The rest of his work consisted of portraits, biblical and allegorical scenes in landscape (figs. 21-24), and quick sketches of friends and surroundings which became an increasingly important part of his *oeuvre*.

By 1928 Evergood had begun a painting which heralded the beginning of his mature work—the double portrait of *M.T. Florinsky, D.S. Mirsky and the Pidget*. The drawings also reflect new interests and new friends. A portrait of Margaret and Helen Shotwell (fig. 26), daughters of Professor James Shotwell, the famous teacher and historian, the double portrait of his father (fig. 25) and that of Chiquita Huara—daughter of the great Peruvian dancer, Helba Huara, whom he had known in Paris (fig. 37), a beautiful academic head of Charles Edward Smith, and many others from this time show the gradual liberation of his drawing technique. He was becoming a master of the peculiarly impatient yet strong line characteristic of his later graphic work, though a virtuoso gracefulness remained which he finally succeeded in purging. The "fumbling" that he so admired in the drawings of Pascin and Rodin had become an integral rather than a self-conscious part of his own expression.

The new strength is apparent in a humorous pencil sketch of *Leah and Tom at Whitestone Landing from the Rear Seat of a Chevrolet,* in which the couple's eyes are seen in the rear-view mirror, and in two ver-

[16]

sions of the double portrait of Charles Edward Smith and Fred Mangold, respectively titled *Two O'Clock* and *Four O'Clock* (figs. 28, 29). Smith remembers that they sat for these in the small Christopher Street studio after a late night listening to jazz. As time wore on, the series of sketches became more linear and more spontaneous. In the final pencil version, compared to the wash drawing, the bulky feet and long-fingered, sensuous and exaggerated hands, the free single line of the bodies and deliberate lack of detail stress the directions Evergood was taking.

III. THE EARLY PRINTS

Evergood has never considered himself a printmaker in any sense of the word, and he has always "drawn on the plate," exploring the intaglio media in only a tentative fashion, even after his exposure to Stanley William Hayter's pioneering experimental studio in Paris. "These early prints were just a few little romantic ideas to try to learn something, the outgrowth of my own little childish creation—the beginnings of me as an artist." A chronological study of the surviving etchings of the twenties and thirties is hampered by the fact that almost none are dated; Evergood's temperament and versatility do not allow precise dating on stylistic grounds.

The early biblical and allegorical prints executed in New York from 1926 to 1929 are technically and compositionally quite conventional, but by the end of this period Evergood had developed a more interesting imagery and treatment which were strictly his own, if remaining within a traditional framework. The first 1926 etching—*Heaven* (fig. 117)—has much in common with the drawing of *Job on the Dunghill*. Delicately drawn but crowded with vigorous forms and strokes, it has a refinement which was modified in succeeding works. *Daughters of Cain* (fig. *119*) is still relatively understated, but *Centaurs and Men* and *Abraham, Isaac, and the Angel* (figs. *118, 120*) are crudely, almost obsessively cross-hatched; the figures are dark and hastily outlined, their volumes flattened. In the four illustrations for Milton's *Lycidas* (figs. *121-26*) this cross-hatching gave way to a heavy dotted outline which was further simplified in the virgins group (figs. *127-29*) of 1928-29.

Stylistically, these etchings are marked by an increasing dependence upon contrast of very fine, faint line against harsh or heavily scored strokes. The center of interest is usually emphasized by deep biting or heavy inking; the background is pale and thinly outlined with no modeling, a method carried through in the late thirties and forties (figs. *155, 157*). As he acquired more technical skill and learned to engrave in Hayter's Paris studio, Evergood found ways to make these contrasts less obvious and to suggest shading and atmosphere in a less heavy-handed manner. The early cross-hatching was replaced by a grainy texture which served the same purpose of emphasis but allowed the forms more buoyancy and endowed the prints with a purer and lighter aspect (figs. *139, 140, 150*).

After 1927, the compositions were usually simple, centered on a frieze-like group of figures, seated, reclining or gravely dancing in a landscape dotted with animals, trees or mountains. Except for the central group, the compositional elements are unsystematically dispersed, as though the artist felt compelled to eliminate design in the generally understood sense. Considering Evergood's mature style, this seems very possible, although perhaps at the time it was unconscious and motivated simply by a desire for more freedom of expression within the limited means he had set himself. This dispersement is also echoed in the isolation of the figures within a single composition. The idealized youths and young girls, with their expressionless faces and rhetorical gestures, either stare directly at the spectator or at a single protagonist, self-consciously ignoring all others present. The resultant hieratic effect and emphasis on the primitive nature of these prints is also reflected in their deliberately static quality. Evergood's interest in Terpsichore was presumably stimulated by his attachment to Julia Cross, but rigid immobility is retained even in *Primitive Dance* (fig. *142*), where a more energetic step is being performed and a galloping horse and running dog add to the momentum. To this day, Evergood's interpretation of movement has continued to be more ritual than realistic.

The female nudes, particularly those in the dance series (figs. *142-44*) of 1930, are strongly reminiscent of Picasso's pre-Cubist drawings of 1906. Since the great Spaniard was as famous then as now, his work was seen everywhere and there is no doubt that Evergood had often been exposed to it. Whether this comprised an actual influence or not is debatable, but it is pertinent to note that the same element of self-assured crudity was found in Picasso's transitional period between the romantic, sensitive Blue Period and the final explosion of his own mature style—Cubism.

At one point around 1928, Evergood interrupted his classical preoccupations to combine them with a gentle pantheism in a lyrical series of small etchings with such titles as *Woodland Romance, Alone with Nature, The Ploughman Homeward Plods His Weary Way, Poetry of Nature,* and so on (figs. *130-35*). They differ from the earlier works in both style and content. Nature, hitherto represented only as a repetitive landscape background, became the focal point, with man (or more often, woman) an incidental figure,

[17]

small and unobtrusive, sunk in contemplation of his surroundings. Most of the figures are in contemporary dress, but occasionally a classical nude reclines nearby. Here again, the figures ignore each other, as though the nudes were romantic phantoms evoked by modern man's twilight musings. The mood in these prints is not wholly romantic or classical. The final impression conveyed by the frozen gestures and ambiguous titles is one of primitive naiveté, as well as that "little sense of mystery" upon which Evergood has always insisted.

This was particularly evident when he departed now and then from the self-imposed norm of the general groups. Working primarily with drypoint, he gained a new effect based upon the opposition of a soft, very fine line and a rich velvety drypoint against white areas in three 1930 works (figs. 146, 148, 149). The result seems luxurious compared to the puritanical harshness of the other prints. In another direction, he reverted to the Slade training which he was struggling to overcome with a more personal style by depicting *Adam and Eve* (fig. 147) in the style of Dürer or Cranach. In *The Phantom Horse* (fig. 136), he utilized a not quite effaced image from an earlier state to create a peculiarly haunting scene. The ghostly rider, slightly larger in scale than the placid figures through which he rushes with apprehensive face, seems to spring from nowhere, bringing a note of supernatural warning to the peaceful group. The theatrical but dreamlike *Drawing on a Wall* (fig. 145) also plays on a double surface; a frieze of strangely unrelated classical figures moves across a pitted, scratched and textured plane. A similar element of fantasy is found in the *Menacing Black Horse* (fig. 146), and the more bucolic *Sick Horse* (fig. 137).

Probably the outstanding print of these years is *The Antique Urn* (fig. 141), an etch-

ing, engraving and drypoint on a brass plate from the bottom of a ship. This was done in Paris around 1930 while Evergood was working occasionally at Hayter's. Knife-like striations and scratchy line define the massive figure which dominates the composition. In spite of the pastoral atmosphere there is a barbaric earthiness about her not found in any of the paper-doll nudes in the other etchings. A second, purely linear nude—a phantom or another self—floats above, holding a flower. This enigmatic ensemble recalls the modern fertility goddesses of the artist's mature work, anticipating the "Evergood Woman" of the fifties—strong, humorous, sensuous, and very much in control of her environment.

Two belated offspring of the classical period must be mentioned here. The 1936 *Centaur is Gone* (or *Footsteps in the Sand*) (fig. 152) is an etching, engraving and drypoint in which Evergood worked with sandpaper over an old photo-engraving plate as though it were a mezzotint, picking up the grays and deepening the rich blacks of the previous surface. The figure smiles enigmatically at the spectator with a sad and knowing look, raising one arm as if in farewell. This did indeed prove to be farewell to all of Evergood's earlier, inward-directed preoccupations. The other etching, *The Encroaching City* of 1938 (fig. 151), although recalling the pastoral series from a decade earlier, marks the first appearance of industrial subject matter in an Evergood print. The weeping willows and the graceful figures are relics of the romantic period, but the smokestacks in the distance are intruders. In an embryonic form they represent the powerful symbols of modern life and oppression which play such a great part in the later work.

IV. SOURCES AND BEGINNING OF MATURE WORK

Among the various influences on Evergood's work at this period, William Blake may have been outstanding as regards the prints. Blake's lack of concern for conventional standards and his mystical, anti-esthetic spirit "embodied poetry, wit, and imagination" for the young artist. It is also important to cite Goya, Daumier, Hogarth and Rowlandson, whose relationship to the later prints and drawings needs no explanation. Then, as now, it was "the mistakes in a man's work that interested me. I don't like it so precise that there are no mistakes. Lautrec had this creative quality, whereas people like Beardsley lacked all guts, took no chances and stood for 'perfection.' The inspiration of men like Lautrec and Modigliani stems not from technique or accident, but from the fresh observance of incidents in their lives. Their experiences seem new and fresh because no one before them had lived just those experiences. Their techniques were very simple—using age-old methods they accomplished their objectives by the liveness of their line, their challenging individual approach to the subject . . . The most essential ingredient for this kind of approach (which I also consider my own) is honesty."

But at the same time, aside from the old masters—especially Grünewald, and the newer masters—especially Toulouse-Lautrec, Degas and Modigliani, there were two modern artists whose contradictory styles made a great impression and have distinct echoes in Evergood's mature development, although absorbed long ago into his personal mode of expression. These are Jules Pascin and Max Beckmann. Evergood remembers being overwhelmed by his first Beckmann exhibition—probably that in New York in 1926. He felt an immediate sympathy for the somber Teutonic

7. Orchestra, (c.1932), charcoal, 11¾ x 19½, the artist.

expressionism, for Beckmann's heavy black outlines, his simplification and use of the close-up, harsh discontinuity of composition and pasty-faced, haunted figures, often drawn from the world of carnival or theatre. But as Evergood has observed, "Although I idolized Beckmann, I didn't get these things *from* Beckmann, I got them from looking at the same people." In direct contrast to Beckmann's tough, insistent contour and acrid color, Pascin's sensuous, hypersensitive tracery, languid figures, good naturedly erotic subject matter and delicate pastel palette provided Evergood with an intermediary step between Degas and Lautrec and the stronger dose of modern figurative art represented by Picasso, Beckmann, and the Americans.

At the end of his three years in New York, in 1929, Evergood had his second one-man show, this time at the Montross Galleries. A quotation from the catalogue indicates how little the work shown there, which included fifteen etchings, reflected the imminent breakthrough: "The poetry and mystery of life is [Evergood's] principal aim. . . . His pictures do not smack of realism, not of what to him is an unimportant striving to portray the life of the day." Yet by the time he reached Paris again in early 1930, Evergood had begun "to think in terms of expression . . . to think of men like Bosch and Breughel. I had seen their work in museums and churches, I knew Gerard David, Cranach, Grünewald, and I realized that they had a great unity with their times, with the kind of people living around them, so I gradually went in their direction. I went even further overboard than some people would have done who hadn't started in the completely separate vein of dreams. I wanted to shock, to wake people up. I said to myself, you're going to be judged on the spiritual values, on what you say about people and life, not just on piddling dreams and im-

[20]

aginations. I got this big jolt, knocking around Europe footloose. I was facing a future of decision. Do you want to be a little dreamer all your life or do you want to be a part of your times, express a little of human values seen in the streets and life around you? I had to break away from Cézanne, from groups of figures for the sake of esthetics. I had to get down to the sour expression on a guy's face who's been starving for two months, so I embarked on this somewhat lonely path of curious invention, introspection and the sudden unfettering into a more outgoing expression dealing with the living organisms of my own day."

Now he began to move away from the almost exclusive preoccupation with graphic media and to become a painter in every sense of the word. At the end of 1930 he and Julia Cross went to Spain where, in Toledo, they found an apartment overlooking El Greco's garden. The exposure to the great Mannerist's work in quantity was a tremendous experience. It convinced Evergood of his own directions and ended the decade of concentration on drawing, leaving him free to become a painter in his own right. Although he was still using mythological and genre themes, his last stay in France had impressed upon him that despite his attraction to the "exciting pioneer work of the Impressionists, Post-Impressionists, Cubists, and some of the more recent experimental groups, nothing seemed applicable to or remotely connected to America in design, color, form or smell. The idea grew slowly within me that the vitality of America was a fitting subject for the brush of a painter. In 1931 this seemed important enough to me to come back to the country of my birth and try to do it. I found that I was one of several painters with similar aims in view. The sum total of my work is divided into two categories, two periods: 1) running away from life, 2) meeting life head-on.''

"Meeting life head-on'' first consisted of what has been called Evergood's "autobiographical period.'' It began with drawings of friends and sketches from life in his own immediate environment rather than with any concern for society's ills. By the time he returned to New York in the summer of 1931 his course was set. He was soon to attempt the "prodigious feat of combining art, modernity and humanity. At thirty years, I was a comparative babe in art for all my academic training. To go from painting imaginative biblical figures to the down-to-earth robustness of a steel worker's boot or his wrinkled salt-caked sweater or his grimy blue-jeans was a big jump, and to me a big challenge.'' He and Julia Cross were married in August and made their precarious living by working in a Gallery of American Indian Art. Evergood continued to draw from the model and to do numerous portrait sketches. *Smiling Julia, Juju in Ballet Costume (figs. 32,33)* and *Julia Painting* show the further decline of his Slade-engrained inhibitions and the beginning of the direct expressionist style for which he is known. More courageous in both image and technique, they also mark the emergence of Evergood from himself toward the world. "In these years I had to re-educate myself. I began to have a new perception of what drawing meant.''

Around this time he came to know John Sloan and his wife Dolly—"a bright little Irish bulldog'' who gave Evergood a great deal of encouragement and affection. He drew her portrait in Child's Restaurant in 1934 on an envelope from the Temporary Emergency Relief Administration, where she worked *(opp.)*. Sloan himself was "genuinely enthusiastic'' about Evergood's work. "He bought a painting, came to the studio . . . inspiring a part of me and my ideals.'' In 1933-34 Evergood met

8. Portrait of Dolly Sloan, 1934, pencil, 9½ x 4⅛, the artist.

Reginald Marsh, whose similar beliefs in reflecting one's own times also had an effect on his choice of subject matter.

Surviving sketches from 1932 include quick notations of political meetings, workers' groups and other signs of this increasing awareness. During the Depression years reminders of the state of the world were all too plentiful and Evergood's response was immediate. In *Bronx Coloseum* (sic) *Rally*— a spontaneous colored chalk study—a red flag waves from the platform and a banner reads "Support Revolutionary Struggles of German Masses." He was still more of an observer than a participant but, significantly, the drawing was done from the platform. Similar sketches show construction workers, street crowds, and meetings. One, scrawled on the back of a program for a costume ball, shows two Negro musicians and a man with a sign reading "Workers, Musicians, Unite."

Music, and jazz in particular, played an important role from around 1932 to 1935. In 1927 Evergood had met Charles Edward Smith, the poet and pioneer jazz historian, who had seen and admired his Dudensing exhibition. They were soon, and still are, fast friends. Through Smith, Evergood was introduced to the Harlem night clubs and to some of the early jazz greats, such as Sidney Bechet, Leadbelly and Jazzbo Collins (see *figs. 46-49*). Visits to the Sugar Cane Club, the Cotton Club and Jerry's Rustic Log Cabin are recorded in quick sketches reflecting the artist's enthusiasm for the music and the surroundings. A portrait drawing of Bechet (*fig. 48*) was made on the musician's birthday at his apartment behind a tailor shop. A guitarist from Fletcher Henderson's orchestra provided the rhythm section as Evergood "improvised with drawing pad and Bechet with soprano sax." Smith remembers that while never interested in the scholarly side of jazz,

Evergood was most involved with its all-enveloping spontaneity. "He liked the kind of jazz that, like the cake in *Alice in Wonderland*, says 'Eat Me.' "[7] In the large canvas, *Music*, of 1933-38, painted for the Pierre Degeyter Club, he expressed his sympathy with the spirit and gusto of the improvisatory hot bands. Undoubtedly this kind of music also appealed to him as a social phenomenon—as the exuberant creative outlet of a subjugated people.

V. SOCIAL AWARENESS: THE THIRTIES

It was also in 1932 that Evergood had an experience which he feels "drove him faster" into social awareness. Walking one winter night down Christopher Street to the Hudson, or "North River," he came upon a shanty town where "the outcasts of New York, the outcasts of civilization, were huddled around a fire made from sticks they picked up around the wharves. The only food they had was from garbage cans." He bought them some gin and went back for drawing materials. "I learned about suffering and the courage of the oppressed and downtrodden that night." The sketches made then and on subsequent occasions of the homeless Negroes with names like Terrapin, Skeezix, Geach, Rakey and Bean Pod (*figs. 43, 44*), had a new power. Evergood's involvement sacrificed niceties of line and composition to a passionate and unequivocal sympathy with the subject at hand. Distortion and crudity were employed deliberately to evoke deep compassion and rebellion against conditions that forced men to live like this. A hard, jagged charcoal or crayon line, coarse crosshatching, a childlike disregard for elegance or design—these were his expressive tools. Several of these drawings, such as *Jungle Dwellers*, *North River* and *Clothes Line Terrapin*

9. Cup of Tea, 1939, brush and ink over pencil,
17 x 11, Lawrence Arine, Rochester.

10. Two Nuns in Hoboken, c.1938, ink, pencil,
crayon, 19¾ x 15⅝ irreg., Mr. and Mrs.
George Rickey, East Chatham, N.Y.

and His Beaver served as the basis for paintings in the W.P.A. period.

From this time on, Evergood threw himself into the life around him. No longer satisfied to record only what he saw, he now recorded what and how he felt as well; his object was to remedy, to make more people see, through his art, what surrounded them. He also realized the necessity of direct action to cure the social evils of his times. He was president of the Artists Union and of the United American Artists, member of the Artists Congress, the Artists Committee of Action, the Artists League of America, and a founding member of Artists Equity. In 1937-38 he was managing supervisor of New York's Easel Division of the Federal Art Project, painted murals for the WPA, and generally gave of himself and his work so wholeheartedly that this long period of activity culminated in complete nervous exhaustion in the mid-forties, when he moved to the country under doctor's orders.

Persecuted in the witch-hunting fifties for "joining the fight against Fascism too early," he was called before the House Un-American Activities Committee as late as 1959. Evergood's art has never been so strictly political as passionately involved.[8] "I am not a political theorist, I am a painter," he insists. "I feel that those who judge art on a basis of conformity, esthetic or political, should recognize the dangers inherent therein. People throughout the world must fight for the complete freedom of the artist to create as he desires and to be judged by his countrymen and by the world solely on his work."

Evergood was always the energetic participator rather than the cerebral explainer. His art, like his statements, reflects a certain political naiveté which belies the subversive intent seen by his adversaries. "Sure I'm a Social Painter," he wrote defiantly in 1943, but

his cause was a general one—humanity, rather than any specific political program. While the social role he accepted is undoubtedly responsible for some of his most powerful work, he is, as John Baur has pointed out, "different from most social protest artists, both in attitude and style. Much of his work is not protest at all, but an affirmation of human values or, occasionally, pure fantasy."[9] These positive elements have saved him from the obsolete and repetitive dullness into which many of the artists associated with him in the forties have fallen. "Evergood's social consciousness . . . is partly an affirmation of the ugly."[10] It has led at times to oversimplified works whose main virtue is their integrity and the undeniably good intentions behind them, leaving him wide open to accusations of overstatement and lack of subtlety. Nevertheless, these exaggerations are the product of Evergood's steadfast honesty. Sometimes he is so honest that he even forgets to be an artist. He has stated proudly that his work should be comprehensible to anyone, that he uses no "abstruse, mystic or inverted symbolism which only the artist can understand." He often speaks and writes against the contemporary trends of conformism to the non-objective. He sees abstraction as an institution which denies its original premises of freedom and ends in stylistic slavery by departing from life.

"Nothing that Evergood does is separate from the heart," Elizabeth McCausland has said.[11] His forthrightness and indignation are far more often effective than not, as in the powerful statement made by *American Tragedy*, an exposé of police brutality in a South Chicago strike against Republic Steel in May, 1937, which was painted partly from newspaper photographs. Evergood himself had participated in the famous "219" strike in 1936, had been beaten and thrown in jail and knew, therefore, of what he was painting. The

[24]

drawing for *American Tragedy* (fig. *45*) is perhaps more directly convincing than the canvas. Where the painting singles out the principal figures and separates the rioting crowd from its environment by a strip of bare land, the drawing is a spontaneous turmoil of gestures, giving the impression of having been executed in the heat of direct reaction. The rapid, sure line, rough cross-hatching and strong contrasts of black and white (with touches of blue and red as well as a collage area) are well suited to the subject. Evergood often achieved this strong sense of immediacy although the scenes depicted had not been observed first hand. The c. 1937 lithograph, *Sorrowing Farmers* (fig. *154*), was also inspired by a newspaper clipping, this time of the Dust Bowl, and studies for *Mine Disaster* were taken from an old book of engravings on Welsh mines (*p. 10*).

VI. DRAWINGS AND PRINTS AS STUDIES FOR PAINTINGS

The emphasis that Evergood has laid on draughtsmanship throughout his career, and the fact that it is a major ingredient of his painting style, accord his graphic work a more important place than it would have in the case of many modern artists. "Drawings," wrote Goethe, "are invaluable, not only because they give in its purity the mental intention of the artist, but because they bring immediately before us the mood of his mind at the moment of creation." This holds more or less true depending on whether the drawing is an "occasional sketch, a preparatory study or a drawing for its own sake," to use Monroe Wheeler's classifications. The direct relationship of Evergood's drawing to his paintings, for example, has greatly varied not only over the decades but from canvas to canvas. Nevertheless, certain clues to the creative process

can be drawn from this variety, and especially from those sketches or drawings which eventually were used either wholly or partially in paintings.

Evergood often does not make detailed studies for a painting, but goes to work instinctively, sketching the main lines of the composition on the canvas in charcoal. However, the general idea for the painting may have been previously explored in drawings made for that purpose, or it may have originated in a drawing first intended only as an independent work of art. When he is embarking on a large-scale project with many figures and complex design, he usually makes a quick pencil working sketch, in which the placement of compositional elements are tentatively mapped out. These small "ideagrams" are not intended as drawings in any esthetic or finished sense and, in fact, are not meant to see the light as separate objects. Luckily, however, some have been retained—the first of which is a preparatory drawing for the 1932 mural *Towards Peace* (fig. *38*), shown that year at the Museum of Modern Art. Comparison with the painting shows how much of the final version "happened" on the canvas rather than in the plan. On the other hand, a larger and more detailed sketch—more of a cartoon in the traditional sense—for the mural, *The Story of Richmond Hill* (fig. *40*), shows the central panel in almost complete form except for background details, although the left panel had not yet evolved at all and the right one was to change considerably. A third drawing from the same period—a dashing brush and ink sketch for one vertical panel of a portable mural—is the product of a much earlier stage of creative planning, the immediate setting down of an idea in the heat of inspiration (*p. 26*).

Such works are exciting simply as gestures of creation. They provide insights into the in-

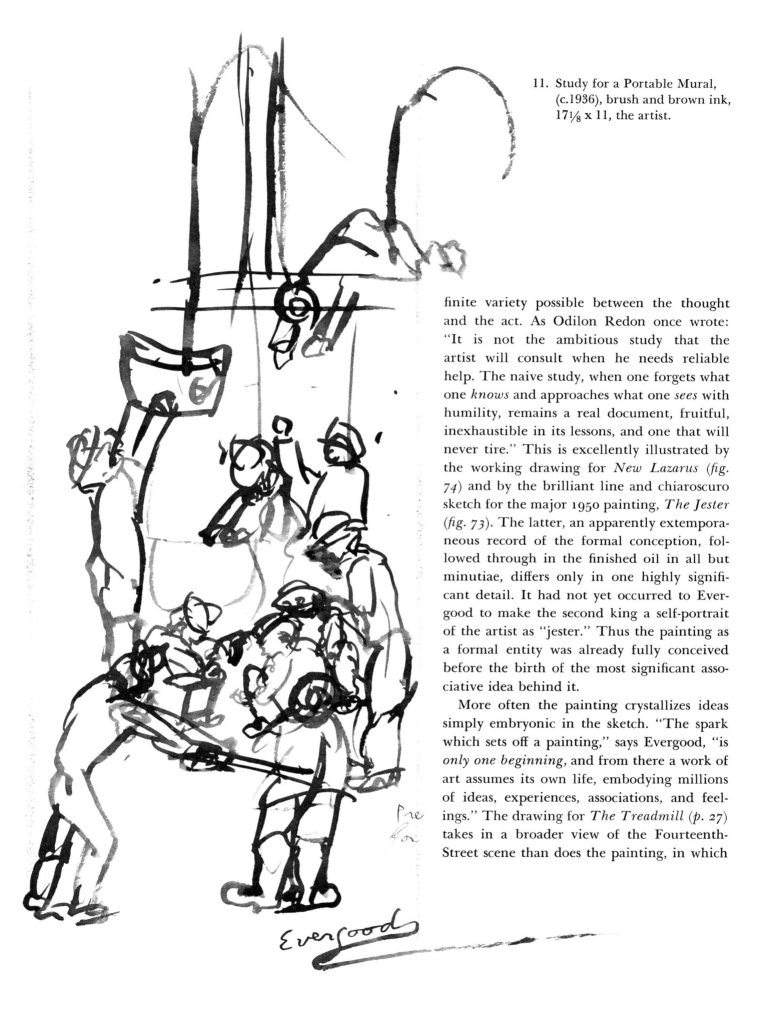

11. Study for a Portable Mural, (c.1936), brush and brown ink, 17⅛ x 11, the artist.

Evergood

finite variety possible between the thought and the act. As Odilon Redon once wrote: "It is not the ambitious study that the artist will consult when he needs reliable help. The naive study, when one forgets what one *knows* and approaches what one *sees* with humility, remains a real document, fruitful, inexhaustible in its lessons, and one that will never tire." This is excellently illustrated by the working drawing for *New Lazarus* (*fig. 74*) and by the brilliant line and chiaroscuro sketch for the major 1950 painting, *The Jester* (*fig. 73*). The latter, an apparently extemporaneous record of the formal conception, followed through in the finished oil in all but minutiae, differs only in one highly significant detail. It had not yet occurred to Evergood to make the second king a self-portrait of the artist as "jester." Thus the painting as a formal entity was already fully conceived before the birth of the most significant associative idea behind it.

More often the painting crystallizes ideas simply embryonic in the sketch. "The spark which sets off a painting," says Evergood, "is *only one beginning,* and from there a work of art assumes its own life, embodying millions of ideas, experiences, associations, and feelings." The drawing for *The Treadmill* (*p. 27*) takes in a broader view of the Fourteenth-Street scene than does the painting, in which

12. Study for "The Treadmill", c.1933, pencil, 13¾ x 10⅞, the artist.

a single facade fills the entire surface with signs, lights and other chaotic demands on the attention of the spectator, who is more effectively surrounded than if he had been allowed to stand back, as in the sketch. This close-up device for increased impact is found in many Evergood paintings, both simple figure compositions and more complex scenes. In the mid-thirties it also fulfilled another function, as the artist was then especially interested in the humorous potential of lettering and signs. A sketch of sailors and girls on the street includes a bar sign: "No hard liquor served to Gobs;" *The Treadmill* advertises "Hobson, the Choice of Millions, the Choice of Millionaires (no connection to Hobson Bay)," and in *Art on the Beach,* a pier in the background is labeled "Promisetown." The sketch for the latter (*fig. 39*) also demonstrates Evergood's continuing interest in the motley "types" of humanity. While its design was barely followed through in the painting, the

notes around the edge were eventually realized in individual figures. They read: "Old Salt, Little He-Man, Big He-Man, He-Woman, Farmers, Sailors Sneering, Adonis, Dowager, Pee Wee, etc."

Just as the wilful distortion of Evergood's mature drawing style was made possible by years of rigorous academic disciplines, so the apparent spontaneity of his paintings is often based on painstaking background research, indicated by numerous pages of detailed studies for the "props." Always conscientious about accuracy, he went to the Museum of Natural History and drew flamingoes in preparation for the 1947 painting, *Flight of Fancy.* In his portfolios one finds sketches of shrimps for *American Shrimp Girl,* insects for *Moon Maiden,* fish for *Dream Catch,* two large sheets of sparrows for the famous *Lily,* as well as miscellaneous objects such as machine parts, a pulley, and anatomical studies, one of which is titled *Stomach Investigation.*

There are also, of course, the "occasional sketches" and drawings concerned with broader conceptions which may precede a painting by years before they are finally used. As Edward Bryant has pointed out, "Evergood is one of those few artists working today whose creative intent has remained so consistent that he is able to return to an idea conceived several years before and bring it to completion."[12] Spontaneous sketches from life eventually incorporated into paintings include the jazz sketches of a pianist—probably Willie the Lion Smith—at Jerry's Rustic Log Cabin, and *Jazzbo Singing,* the North River Jungle group, and the numerous portrait drawings of Charles Edward Smith from 1928 on, which can be considered as preliminary sketches for *Evening Reading*—the 1934 painting of him and his wife. Two early drawings show Smith in the contemplative mood and reclining position of the

13. Insect Studies (detail), (c.1944), blue ink, 10½ x 5⅜, the artist.

painting. These can be called studies in a more narrow sense, although they precede the canvas by as much as four years in one case (*fig. 36*); in the other case the second figure is not Smith's wife but Evergood's (*fig. 41*). There are also instances of drawings being executed *after* the painting, such as *The Indestructibles* of 1946 (*fig. 68*), which follows the oil in every detail except for a slight difference in scale. The subject was the Spanish political prisoners still incarcerated as a result of the civil war, "still reading, still alive, still with a little hope." The drawing was made for a souvenir program of a benefit theater performance, one of many such donations to charity events for causes close to Evergood's heart and to his art.

Another category of "studies" includes those finished drawings which are found almost detail for detail in paintings and may have either preceded or succeeded the canvases. *Watching the Parade* (*fig. 52*) has its counterpart in the painting *Whither America*. Following his usual practice, Evergood made the painting more close-up, strengthening and simplifying the composition by using only the top half of the drawing and omitting one figure, but making no essential changes in the central grouping. Other examples of this process are found in his later prints. *Ice Cream Cones for Three* (*fig. 162*) was done before the 1946 painting of the same title, which is an almost exact replica of it. This is the only soft-ground etching Evergood has made, and the technique allowed him to approximate closely the toned pencil drawing. Three primary states of the print show how he worked from line into soft-ground and then sharpened the rather fuzzy image into the final version.

In *Still Life* of 1944 (*fig. 156*) he reversed the process and made a lithograph after a painting. While the central area—the two figures

14. Sketch in Jerry's Rustic Log Cabin (detail), (c.1935), pencil, 7⅞ x 10⅜, the artist.

and the flowers—are the same in both media, he purposefully made the lithograph more vitriolically satirical and more topical. The figures are seen from a greater distance and more detail is included—most importantly, a copy of *The New York Times* with Pearl Harbor blazoned across the headlines. The capitalist couple, who also appear in a 1939 drawing (*p. 23*) and a painting, ignore the news as they pick at their luxurious breakfast beside the enormous, ironically fertile bouquet. Their faces are openly caricatured and

[29]

the title seems to apply less to the flowers than to the figures.

The other prints of the thirties and forties, while not specifically studies for or after paintings, relate to the painted *oeuvre* in their preoccupation with social subject matter. They include *What Price Glory (fig. 153)*, which recalls several "slum paintings" of the late thirties, and the etchings *Portrait of a Miner (fig. 157)* and *Aftermath of War (fig. 155)* in which the play of a dark central group against a blank background with a few pale line figures technically recalls the 1928-30 etchings. In all of these, despite his skill, Evergood continued to be less interested in printmaking innovations than in the most expressive means of transferring his emotion to paper. "I like all the printmaking media in different moods and at different times," he says, "but lithography appeals more to my nature today—it is more like painting, less involved in mechanical and technical processes which kind of bore me, more fluid and spontaneous."

This is borne out by the recent series of lithographs in 1960 and 1961. They are Evergood's most successful graphic work so far. Three are excellent self portraits *(figs. 166-68)* and two are after paintings: *Success Team (fig. 165)* and *Cool Doll in Pool (fig. 164)*. *Success Team* is again concerned with the greedy capitalist, who now guzzles a toast to his amorous success in an atmosphere of sweetness and light, flowers and jewels, which contrasts with the degenerate, sly faces. *Cool Doll* remains very close to the painting, but there is an increased animation in the girl's face and a stress on decorative quality. These prints are drawn in a sinuous and easy line, more spontaneous, more humorous than the paintings, as though the exacting work in oil had freed the hand and mind for the less restricted and more pleasurable act of drawing.

[30]

VII. LANDSCAPE, STILL LIFE AND ILLUSTRATION

Pure landscape has never held much attraction for Evergood, due to his preoccupation with humanity in every form. The landscapes in which the early prints were set are for the most part vague and repetitive; of the group that was pantheistic in intent *(figs. 130-35)*, only the tiny *Bridge* omitted the figure entirely. Several landscape paintings do exist, some of which are very beautiful and recall the romanticism of the early years, and some of which reflect Evergood's interest in the cheerless urban or industrial environments. But the lack of landscape sketches, contrasted with the abundance of comment on his fellow humans, is significant, especially since he has been living in the country, and such scenic country, since the mid-forties.

The year 1940-41, when Evergood was resident artist at Kalamazoo College, seems to have been one of his few periods of even slight involvement with landscape. During that year he made an etching, a zincograph, and a chalk drawing *(figs. 158-61)* of the same subject—the meeting of rural and industrial areas on the outskirts of a midwestern town. In a way it is an extension of the earlier, romantic etching, *The Encroaching City (fig. 151)*, in which the small figures are foils to the environment. Of the three media used in Kalamazoo the zincograph was most suited to the subject, its grainy, smoky quality better evoking the bleak atmosphere. Most effective of the series is a night version called *City Lights (fig. 158)*, where an occasional highlight pierces the velvety curtain that has fallen over the scene, and the deserted night is made more poignant by the lonely figure silhouetted against the window of "Lou's Lunch."

At this time Evergood seems to have been preoccupied also with the motif of man in his environment—the single figure posed before his home, place of work or typical landscape—as in the 1941 drawings *The Hunter* and *Factory Man* (*figs. 53, 54*) or the paintings *The Big Noise* and *My Forebears were Pioneers*. The firm, rounded volumes of the drawings, lovingly defined and modeled and lacking the wrinkles and jagged lines which are usually favorite Evergoodian devices, recall Brueghel the Elder. They belong to one of Evergood's periodic returns to a more classic vision. The soft pencil technique and documentary approach are also found in the illustrations commissioned by *Fortune* in 1945 on the cotton industry (*fig. 60*). There he explored the South through the faces and gestures of the men who work there. At its most successful this series goes beyond reportage and provides a searching portrait of a particular group of Americans and their ways of life. Another series of worker drawings commissioned in 1961 shows the development of Evergood's ideas in the ensuing years. He was no longer as interested in specific type as in the individual face or stance. The recent drawings of man and shovel, woman and rake (*figs. 92, 88*) become portraits rather than objective illustrations. The 1960 and 1961 versions of the man-in-his-environment theme are likewise more humorous and more gently satirical than those of 1941. *Suburban Twilight* (*fig. 91*) was inspired by a scene on the main street of Cedar Falls, Iowa: "a clerkish type, like the little bookkeeper in Gogol's *Overcoat*, but an American version, a little man who lived in a shack by the dump and wore a schoolboy's loud shirts, walking his ancient little dog all alone." The bawdy *joie de vivre* of *The Happy Truckman* (*fig. 93*) tells its own story, as does the jagged line and obsessive detail of *Birth*, one of eight drawings on "A Miner's Life" commissioned by *Mainstream* in 1947 (*fig. 62*).

In the American tradition of the artist-reporter (Homer, Sloan, Luks, etc.), Evergood is a master illustrator. In the best senses of the word such drawings as those discussed above are illustration. They have a point to make, a condition to describe; their anecdotal qualities are mitigated by the fierce intensity of expression. Evergood's training in draughtsmanship stands him in good stead; he is capable of an almost effortless fidelity to observed fact while actually concentrating on the most powerful way of translating those facts into a work of art. As he has said in regard to his oils, "a painting can have all the abstract forces at work, all the electric aliveness of a personal calligraphic line of sensitiveness and strength—and at the same time tell a story or make a statement." Aside from his work for *Fortune* in the 1940's and various miscellaneous commissions (such as *Australia* for the Container Corporation), Evergood has actually illustrated only two books—a sad waste of talent which would not have happened in Europe, with its fondness for luxury editions. The 1929 *Lycidas* (*figs.

15. Soldier, (c.1942), brush and ink, 19¾ x 12⅞, the artist.

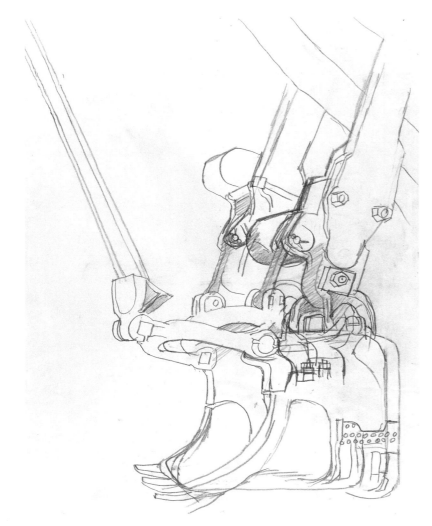

16. **Big Shovel at Mesabi Mines**, (1955), pencil, 24⅜ x 18⅝, the artist.

in most of his figure work. On the other hand, there is one object that has stirred Evergood over the years, and that is the machine. Powerful pencil drawings of machines exist from 1932 on. Some were used in paintings and come under the heading of research sketches, but many stand by themselves among the most abstract works he has done, as though, in spite of himself, he had been affected by the machine age esthetic of such artists as the Futurists or Léger. The great difference is that Evergood, far from idolizing the machine, sees it as a monster to be tamed by man rather than as a symbol of twentieth-century virtues. In his work the monster is a domestic one and he enjoys the sight of a good man professionally manipulating a good machine. The sheer size seems to fascinate him and even the smallest sketches have an impressive breadth and scale. "Men and Machines" is the title of several works, none more important than those executed in 1955 at the Mesabi Iron Mines in Minnesota (*fig. 79*). Evergood was the first artist allowed down into the pit and a man had to stay with him all day to see that he did not stumble over wires that would set off the great charges of dynamite. Of the many sketches he did of the giant bulldozers biting out huge chunks of red and yellow earth, this is the only entire detailed drawing completed in the mine itself. The stupendous size of the operation is conveyed by a bold, insistently space-filling approach; the precision and discipline necessary for its fulfillment are evoked by the contrast between detailed pattern and broad, free rendition.

VIII. THE PORTRAIT

The major part of Evergood's recent work has been devoted to the portrait in one form or another, but "facial expression, the 'fleet-

121-26) was followed in 1951 by an anthology of Gogol's *Russian Stories*. Although Chekhov is Evergood's favorite Russian author, Gogol was a good choice. The illustrations provide a robust accompaniment to his satire, pathos and humor (*figs. 66, 67*).

Pure still life has been as neglected as landscape in Evergood's work. I know of only one recent drawing strictly concerned with objects (*p. 150*). It is a graceful, restrained rendition (although the fruits resemble the hard little breasts of some of his women) lacking the strong inner necessity so obvious

ing, mysterious mirror of mood and character' has always played a larger role in his work than in that of most contemporary painters."[13] He has a fierce compassion, or at times a ferocious dislike, for his protagonists. It is in his portraits that Evergood's attitudes emerge most clearly. He sees everything in extremes. "On one hand we see gluttony and self-aggrandizement," he wrote several years ago, "and on the other self-abnegation, sacrifice, generosity and heroism in different members of the same human race. . . . When a man is dead it only matters if he leaves something acid and something sweet behind him." And in a 1964 radio interview: "I'm only interested in nice human beings and nasty human beings."

What Jack Tworkov once called a "positive attitude" is evident in the way Evergood draws "with great devotion the minutiae of fingernails and wrinkles, eyelids and nostrils. He distorts freely, but avoids boneless generalizations."[14] Like most strong and self-contained artists, in his mature years Evergood has transformed all of his portrait subjects into "Evergoods." Sly faces, large eyes, predatory little mouths, with pointed teeth, expressively distorted hands and feet, "iron breasts," and solid flesh are the most characteristic elements, but the likeness is always retained. A portrait is a direct confrontation between artist and sitter and the successful result combines the essence of both. The sitter is transformed by the artist just as the artist changes with every subject. The various people he has encountered in a lifetime of experience enrich and alter his vision and to each portrait he brings the sum total of this experience. The extreme sensitivity of Evergood's early portraits (figs. 19, 20, 34) acquired depth when his drawing style matured and caught up with his thought process. The 1937 Boy with an Apple (fig. 57), despite its

smooth and subdued handling, has the haunted quality of a Lily and the Sparrows. The model was the hydrocephalic son of a British astronomer Evergood had visited in 1923. Almost fifteen years later, he reinterpreted the drawings he had done then into this strange and yearning portrait. Technical understatement serves to heighten the disturbing pathos created by the boy's half-smile, sidelong glance and the gesture with which he holds the apple gently to him.

His choice of subjects illustrates Evergood's delight in contradictory natures. Three years later he did a large, spontaneous drawing of an older woman with a cigarette (fig. 50), which, though entirely different, is also "typical" according to Evergood's rule of contrasts. The wandering, pressured line disregards actual appearance or scale but succeeds in defining the calm, somewhat cynically amused expression of the sitter. In the 1945 drawing of the late Mabel Dobkin (fig. 64), the texture of the striped sweater is contrasted to the bare skin, the great bulky limbs and unkempt appearance to the figure's pervasive grace and melancholy good humor. Ex-Baseball Pro (fig. 56) is a straightforward and sympathetic portrait of a high class bootlegger who was a business executive and machine politician, and extremely proud of having played professional baseball.

Continually attracted to ugliness, to the odd and to the pathetically unattractive, Evergood has done many studies which border on caricature, such as the noble-ugly-beautiful face of the 1941 Hero, study for a later painting, and the 1954 Girl Reading (fig. 69), where distortion is also anecdotally employed but in a more amusing fashion. The bare bulb, the "girl's" lined face and spectacles, are contrasted with her innocently flowing hair and pathetic nude body poised over the book where solace is only to be found

[33]

for the mind. The portrayal is humorous, but warmly compassionate.

On the other hand, Evergood periodically returns to an extremely classical approach, an example of which is the quietly meticulous *Dear Aunt Susie.* "At this point I felt I needed discipline. It always pops up with me because I think that the real secret of an artist accomplishing something lies in change —from daring splashes to hard discipline within himself. It's the same in the *life* of a sincere artist. There are periods of great abstinence, when he may live like a celibate and feel the need to be purified; then there are also periods of decadence when he is revolting against the society he finds around him. The contrasts make a man's art interesting. Too many artists are only one person. The greatest painters were both."

Sometimes this theory of necessary dualism shows up in a single drawing, such as *Three Little Girls (fig. 87).* The child on the left is wearing stylishly pointed and buckled high-heeled grown-up shoes which are not only a shock in contrast to her innocent face, but to the ordinary tennis shoes worn by the other two, older, subjects. This Lolita touch is a provocative and unexpected element in an otherwise "straight" portrait of three charming children. Different approaches to similar subjects can be found in comparing two other portraits of adolescent girls. *Miss Barzansky in Summertime (fig. 85),* a poignant portrayal of a plump schoolgirl, is executed in a soft and sensuous technique that reflects the moody discontent of an adolescent summer. *Girl in a Swivel Chair,* which was awarded a special prize for drawing at the 1961 Pennsylvania Academy Annual, shows a young dancing pupil of Mrs. Evergood's. Poised and graceful, she represents the other pole of adolescence. "For the first time in a long time I tried to do something pretty.

[34]

Generally I have a contempt for the pretty and am a little ashamed of it, but in this case she *was* so pretty and doll-like that I thought that *was* her character. . . . I admire the ability of Otto Dix, Grosz, even Beckmann, to do pretty people as well as ugly people. They had that charm, to make a woman or a child beautiful."

Three other recent portraits of women must complete this discussion, for which examples are endless. The 1959 *Terry Dintenfass (fig. 83)* shows a lively, positive woman of the world portrayed somewhat wistfully in a clear, uncomplicated pencil line. *Dream Girl Dreaming (fig. 1)* is a wash drawing in which the simple, fluid brush stroke augments the languor of the pose and reflects the tender sensuality with which the Negro model is depicted. The third drawing, *Old Woman (fig. 97),* takes its strength from a single "life-line" which runs diagonally up the page, vitalizing the downcast eyes and passively crossed hands.

Evergood's dependence upon a vital dichotomy in his drawing styles is largely responsible for the fact that his art has remained so alive. He can still whisper and he can still shout. Nowhere is his versatility so much in evidence as in the many portraits of his wife. Julia Evergood has naturally been a recurrent subject over the years. Some drawings of her are pure and sharply delineated. Others are brushed in bold, harsh strokes. Still others are exquisitely detailed and modeled. All reflect an enigmatic personality. Julia appears as sylph and leprechaun, dryad and witch, often touched by an elusive note of cynicism and disillusionment.

Evergood has always been aware of the sacrifices she has made in her dancing career and just how much "Julie's looks, character, discipline, gnome-like quality as a dancer had and have a big effect on my work and life." Four early portraits of 1931-32 *(figs. 32, 33)* show a wistful gamin girl, the dedicated dancer. Her profession, which she still teaches today, has always interested Evergood. In the thirties students of Martha Graham posed for him and in a c.1942 drawing of Mikhail Mordkin (*fig. 70*), with whom Julia has performed, he skilfully captured the simultaneous strength and delicacy of the dancer's gesture. He always seems to choose the proud, awkward stances just preceding or succeeding grace, the off-stage moments, rather than the more obviously beautiful finished product, just as Degas, Lautrec and Rodin did before him.

During the later thirties and forties, Julia appeared only occasionally, although Evergood's women seem to reflect his wife's face or mannerisms in one way or another. His artistic interests then were focused on outside events. But by the mid-fifties intimate portraits claimed more of his time. They share the qualities John Baur has found in Evergood's work of the last decade: "a certain mellowness, a new maturity. . . . The black and white moral values and violence of feeling . . . have yielded to symbolism or satire tempered by detachment, even perhaps by a certain indulgence for human weakness."[15] One of the most popular drawings he has ever done is the 1955 *Woman with the Hair* (*fig. 82*). The great lyrical cloud of hair, from which the wide-eyed face peers hopefully, took him a week to do, "over and over until the paper almost wore away," he recalls, "while the rest of the figure was done in minutes."

Beginning in 1960, the portrait became a major outlet. "I'm plugging away especially on drawing lately," he wrote in 1961, when he was doing a large and important group of "Juju drawings" (*figs. 2, 3, 96, 98*). In most of these she appears with her dogs Coppelia or Puck—perverse Evergoodian animals with sharp little teeth, aureoles of fuzzy hair and expressions that combine the sweet and the diabolical. Among the most penetrating of these studies is *Conversation* of 1961 (*fig. 96*), where the weary eyes and youthful gestures are caught with great psychological insight. In another drawing Julia appears as a young girl in a ponytail staring proudly ahead; in another she is seen in a relaxed mood, softly pensive, her figure drawn in curving lines which are contrasted to the spiky scribble of the dog's back and the great twisted hand that speaks of a certain unease (*fig. 98*). In one strikingly decorative drawing (*fig. 2*), ragged patches of dry brush trace a bold and erratic pattern over the surface, stressing hair, eyes, kimono, hands. In every drawing Julia Evergood is a different person, and yet she is always unmistakably herself in the mixture of toughness and child-like appeal.

IX. RECENT WORK

Related to the portraits are a series of recent works which are calmer, which often have an unashamed tendency toward sentiment, though Evergood deplores realistic "pot-boilers, picture postcard 'art works' whose aroma is just as sweetly nauseating as rose petals sprinkled profusely on a too-long unburied corpse." The sentimental aspects are a major obstacle to an understanding of Evergood's art in this heyday of non-objectivity (and not only abstraction, but classical, hard-edge abstraction). When his occupation with violent protest diminished, his satire became broader, a natural result of such a tempestuous career. Evergood is no longer an angry young man and his art has spread to a more personal and at the same time more far-reaching humanism. His energies are directed less to topical events than to life in general.

This has repeatedly led him to turn to the subject of children and of the mother and child or father and son. In these tranquil pictures, portrayed with a muted tenderness untainted by exaggeration or vulgarity, the emphasis is on faces and hands almost to the exclusion of other motifs. The tendency was clear in 1957 with a classical *Mother and Child (fig. 81)* in which the two forests of fingers provide a foil to the upright postures and clear calm gazes. Two versions of *Two Mothers* from 1961 *(fig. 90)* are made up of faces and hands arranged in a network of light and shadow, line and modeling, angular and circular forms. In *Playing Ball (fig. 101)* the accent is on the perpetually moving hands; in *Father and Son (fig. 89)* it is on the gnarled hand of the father as juxtaposed against the son's smooth face, and on the son's strong hand set against the old man's lined features.

Evergood's most recent works seem to have been executed more rapidly, even more directly and exuberantly than ever before, to a point which might be called raucous. At the same time they are often more esthetically satisfying, more concerned with design and technical finesse. They occasionally display a certain nostalgia for the dramatic commitment of the past, evident in such subjects as *Young Man Home from Work (fig. 110)* which shows a tired worker embraced by his nude wife, but while the theme of the worker may be an old one, a pungent humor has been added.

This particular brand of humor has always been a major part of Evergood's work. Whether based on satire or on a belly laugh, it is as honest and forthright as the man himself, and is part of his thoroughly romantic outlook, often tinged with a Rabelaisian sensuality. He feels that his art has been "affected by the kind of humor about sex that Goya sometimes had, or Rowlandson and Hogarth. I laugh quite often at the use of it that high-pressure advertising makes in the world today.

But I'll be frank, I'm never laughing at the sensuousness of a beautiful woman. I like it." The nude has always figured prominently in his art and it has undergone as many transformations as his other subjects. They range from academic studies in which he sees the body objectively, to others in which he sees it with great compassion as the aging carcass of humanity. Sometimes it is pathetically amusing, but most often he delights in its grace and formal beauty. No matter how freely he distorts the nude body, something of its grandeur remains *(fig. 84)*.

Related to Evergood's earthy humor is his fantasy. The two are combined in such recent drawings as *Dance of the Fishbones, Chairmen of the Bored, Gwathmey Clowning on the Beach*, and the startling *Carpaccio and the Dudas (figs. 104, 105, 102, 111)*. In a broader sense it applies to the violence of *Charred Home and Old Sow with Her Litter (fig. 108)*. All of these have a kind of fearless brutality tempered by a sense of wonder and hearty laughter, a marvelously preposterous quality which has not been so evident in Evergood's work for some time. This note of fantasy which periodically leavens his realism is difficult to define. It emerges in early prints such as *Phantom Horse (fig. 136)*, in portraits like *Boy with Apple (fig. 57)*, in group scenes like *The Jester (fig. 73)* and in drawings like *Strange Birds (fig. 80)*. Even at its most bitterly satirical or grotesque, it is definitely not Surrealism, as has sometimes been declared. There is none of the macabre or self-conscious soul-searching that marks the art of the minor Surrealists, nor any of the provocative insights into the depths of the mind that marks the art of the major Surrealists. Harry Salpeter was right when he described a painting of Evergood's as having "something of that curious archaic feeling in the atmosphere that one discovers as the paradoxical common denominator of most of the works of the Surrealists, but with nothing of the Surrealist manner."[16] They have in common only a certain unpredictability, most often a result of their dissimilar uses of child art and the romantic imagination. Child art is not a predetermined source for Evergood as it is for the Surrealists and the *art brut* of Dubuffet, but a part of the artist's characteristic immediacy and unpremeditated reactions.

Evergood's fantasy is not iconographically complicated, and is unburdened by deeper meanings or obscure symbolism. It is rather, as Baur has pointed out, "a kind of violence of the imagination which sees everything larger than life and responds with a special intensity of feeling."[17] In this sense it is also purely American—naive and not particularly lucid, a little crude in its determination not to be slick. It is as "unsophisticated" as that of Chagall, but closer to earth, to contemporary life. Evergood is able to inject this note as effectively into a social subject as into a portrait, but his fantasy is non-specific and its occasional appearances are purely spontaneous.

Thus a renewed humor, fantasy, and assurance, evident in choice of subject matter and technique, are the characteristics of Evergood's latest graphic works. There is a new element of intensity, a strength and energy of gesture and a new breath of life which strikes a note of youth. Evergood is taking risks a less emphatic person at his age would have left far behind, and by making these risks good, he proves his undiminished creative vitality.

NOTES

1. Charles Edward Smith, *bibl. 51,* p.6.
2. Una E. Johnson, *bibl. 193,* p.5.
3. Quotations from the artist, drawn primarily from conversations with the author, occasionally from his earlier writings, will not be further sourced.
4. In John I. H. Baur's comprehensive biographical essay, *bibl. 31.*
5. Anonymous text in *William von Schlegell,* exhibition catalogue, Art Students League, New York, Oct. 20-Nov. 6, 1952, p.3.
6. Lloyd Goodrich in *Catalog of an Exhibition of the Work of George Benjamin Luks,* Newark Museum, Oct. 30-Jan. 6, 1934, p.12.
7. Charles Edward Smith, in conversation with the author.
8. Evergood did only one actual political cartoon, which was published in *New Masses, bibl. 208.*
9. John I. H. Baur, *bibl. 99,* p.113-114.
10. Fairfield Porter, *bibl. 48,* p.55.
11. *Bibl. 86.*
12. Edward Bryant, *bibl. 87,* p.22.
13. John I. H. Baur, *bibl. 31,* p.58.
14. Jack Tworkov, *bibl. 54,* p.3.
15. John I. H. Baur, *bibl. 31,* p.103.
16. Harry Salpeter, *bibl. 50,* p.75.
17. John I. H. Baur, *bibl. 99,* p.114.

Drawings

NOTE: The following selections from Evergood's many drawings were made with an eye to variety of subject matter, technique, and date. Certain well-known drawings have therefore been omitted in favor of others not previously published. Dimensions are listed in inches and pertain to the full sheet unless given as "sight," in cases where the drawing could not be unframed. Height precedes width. Dates in parentheses do not appear on the drawing itself. A few works were misdated in the past by the artist, and have been corrected by him for the captions. The owner's name is at the end of each caption. L.R.L.

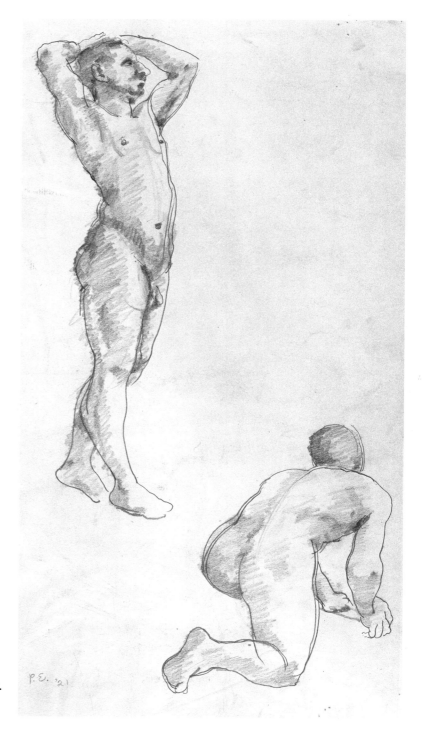

17. Male Model, 1921, pencil, 17⅝ x 13½, the artist.

Job on the dung hill
Philip Evergood '25

Philip Evergood 1925

18. Job on the Dunghill, 1925, pen and ink, 9⅜ x 9, the artist.

19. Portrait of Father, 1922, pencil, 9¾ x 10, Terry Dintenfass, New York.

20. Portrait of Mother, (c.1922), pencil and colored chalks, 12⅜ x 10, Terry Dintenfass, New York (misdated by the artist).

21. Variation on a Classical Theme I, (c. 1927), watercolor over pencil,
15¼ x 16½ sight, Mr. and Mrs. John Davies Stamm, New York.

23. The Burning, Fiery Furnace, (c.1927), watercolor over pencil, 11 x 17, Sidney Bergen, New York.

22. Variation on a Classical Theme II, (c. 1927), watercolor over pencil,
15¼ x 16½ sight, Mr. and Mrs. John Davies Stamm, New York.

24. The Blind Virgins (Theme for a Dance), 1927, pen and ink, wash, and pastel,
23¾ x 18, Mr. and Mrs. John Davies Stamm, New York.

25. Two Studies of Father, 1928, pencil,
11⅞ x 9½, Joseph H. Hirshhorn, New York.

26. Margaret and Helen Shotwell and Friend,
1928, pencil, 18½ x 14½,
Mr. and Mrs. Sol Fishko, New York.

27. Portrait of Anne Feinberg, 1928, pencil,
13⅜ x 10, The Museum of Modern Art,
New York, gift of Mr. and Mrs. William
Feinberg, the donors retaining life interest.

28. Two O'Clock, (1929), brown ink and
wash over pencil, c. 22 x 16,
Charles Edward Smith, New York.

29. Four O'Clock, (1929), pencil, 22 x 16½, Lucy Lippard Ryman, New York
     (misdated by the artist at time of inscription, 1964).

30. Simone, (1924), sepia ink and wash,
   20 x 13⅛, Alexander Dobkin, New York.

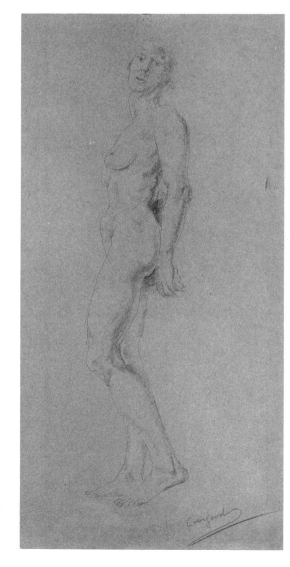

31. Standing Nude, (c.1932), pencil, 19¾ x 12,
   Mr. and Mrs. Warren Brandt, New York.

32. Smiling Julia, (1931), pen and ink, 13⅜ x 11¾, Terry Dintenfass, New York.

33. Juju in Ballet Costume, 1931, charcoal, pen and ink, wash, 21¾ x 14⅝, Joseph H. Hirshhorn, New York.

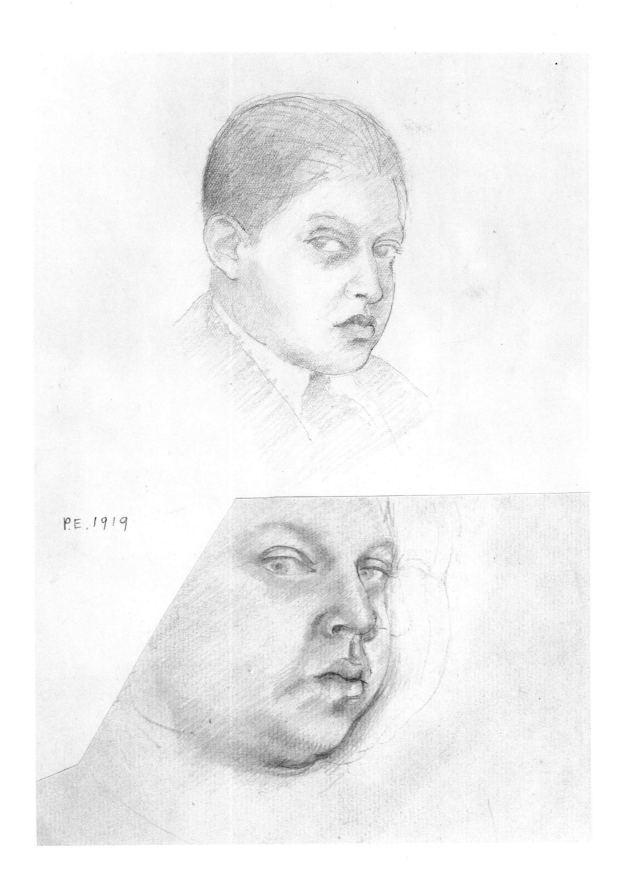

P.E. 1919

34. Two Self Portraits, (upper) 1919 and (lower) 1924, pencil, 12⅝ x 8¾, Mr. and Mrs. George Rickey, East Chatham, N.Y.

35. Study of Girl and Cats, 1930, brush and ink, 14⅞ x 22¼,
Los Angeles County Museum of Art, Maybury Memorial Collection.

36. The Sick Poet (Charles Edward Smith), 1930, pencil, 14¼ x 21, Ida and Moses Soyer, New York.

37. Young Peruvian Dancer (Chiquita Huara), (c.1929), pencil, 22⅝ x 18,
    Joseph H. Hirshhorn, New York (misdated by the artist).

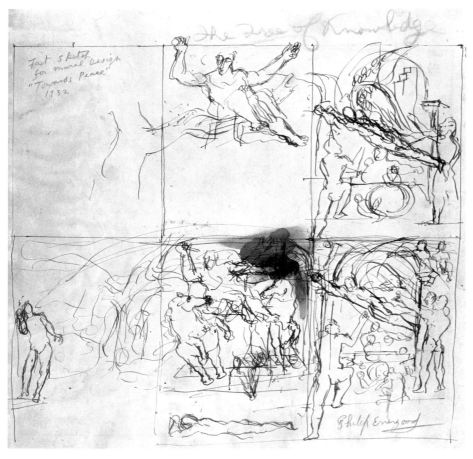

38. Study for "The Tree of Knowledge, Towards Peace" mural, 1932,
pen and ink over pencil, 17¼ x 12¾ irreg., the artist.

40. Study for "The Story of Richmond Hill" mural, (1935), ink, pencil, collage, 12½ x 42, the artist.

Sailors Brazen
Adonis
the Dowager
Pee wee etc.

Old Salt
Little He-man
Big He-man
He-woman
Farmers

Phil Evergood

39. Study for "Art on the Beach", (c.1936), pencil, 7 x 14¼ irreg., the artist.

41. In a Woodstock Cabin, (c.1932), pen and ink, pencil, crayon, wash, 18½ x 22¼, Milton Brown, New York.

42. Lynching Party, 1935, pencil, 21 x 26½, Joseph H. Hirshhorn, New York.

43. Rakey and Camp Cook, Jungle Dwellers,
1932, 14⅝ x 10¾, the artist.

44. North River Jungle, 1933, pencil, 18½ x 22¾, Joseph H. Hirshhorn, New York.

45. Study for "American Tragedy", 1937, red and blue crayon, ink and wash,
pencil, collage, 15½ x 22⅝, Ida and Moses Soyer, New York.

To Joe Foster
in Friendship
P.E.

47. Sketch for "Jerry's Rustic Log Cabin",
    Harlem (Willie the Lion Smith?), 1935,
    pencil, 7⅞ x 10⅜, Julia Evergood, New York.

46. Sketch for "Jazzbo Singing", November 1933,
    pencil, blue ink, 10⅜ x 7⅞, Julia Evergood,
    New York.

49. Home Jam Session with Don Freeman, 1933
    (reworked 1965), pencil, pen and ink,
    watercolor and collage, 10½ x 8,
    Julia Evergood, New York.

50. Woman With Cigarette, 1940, pencil, 10⅞ x 16½, Joseph H. Hirshhorn, New York.

48. Sidney Bechet, 1934, pencil, pen and blue ink,
13⅞ x 10⅛, Julia Evergood, New York.
(Inscribed by Bechet.)

51. The Drawing Lesson, 1936, blue crayon, 17¼ x 12, Mr. and Mrs. John Davies Stamm, New York.

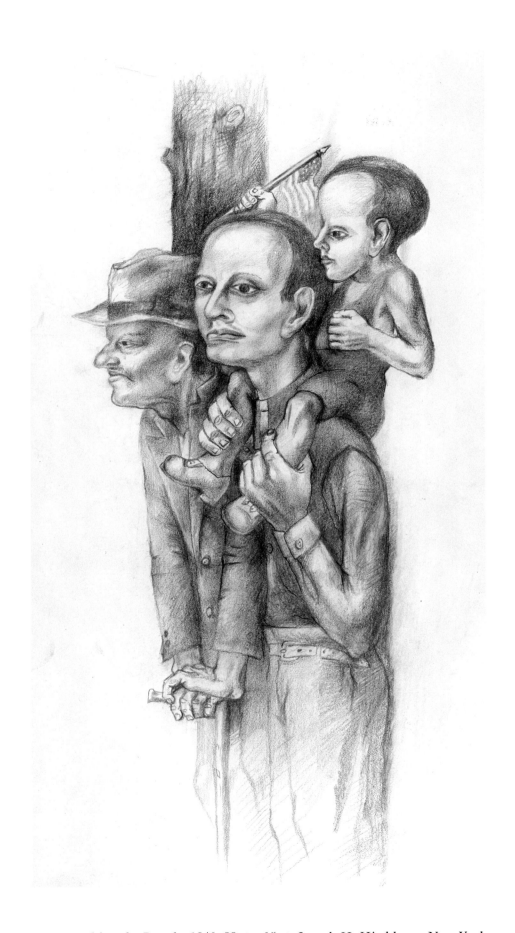

52. Watching the Parade, 1940, 22½ x 15⅜, Joseph H. Hirshhorn, New York.

53. Hunter, 1941, pencil, 17¼ x 23¼, Joseph H. Hirshhorn, New York.

54. Factory Man, 1941, pencil, 13⅜ x 16, Mr. and Mrs. Chaim Gross, New York.

55. Horizons, (c.1936), ink and wash, 19¾ x 16, Ida and Moses Soyer, New York.

56. The Ex-Baseball Pro, 1947, 11⅞ x 19⅝ sight, Allen R. Hite Art Institute, Louisville, Ky.

57. Boy With an Apple, 1937, pencil, 17¾ x 11⅜, Joseph H. Hirshhorn, New York.

58. Fishing Industry, 1944, pencil, 19 x 24, Miss Katherine Gwathmey and Miss Ida Tarrington Gwathmey, New York.

59. Radioland, 1948, ink and gouache, 19⅛ x 20⅞, Ida and Moses Soyer, New York.

60. Dominoes, 1945, pencil and white oil wash, 18½ x 23¾, Mr. and Mrs. David Holtzmann, New York. (Commissioned for *Fortune,* Nov. 1945.)

61. Removing a Diseased Gall Bladder, 1944, pencil, 18¼ x 22⅝, Frank and Lidia Kleinholz, Port Washington, N.Y.

62. Birth I, 1947, colored inks, pen, brush and wash, 19¾ x 25⅝, Joseph H. Hirshhorn, New York.

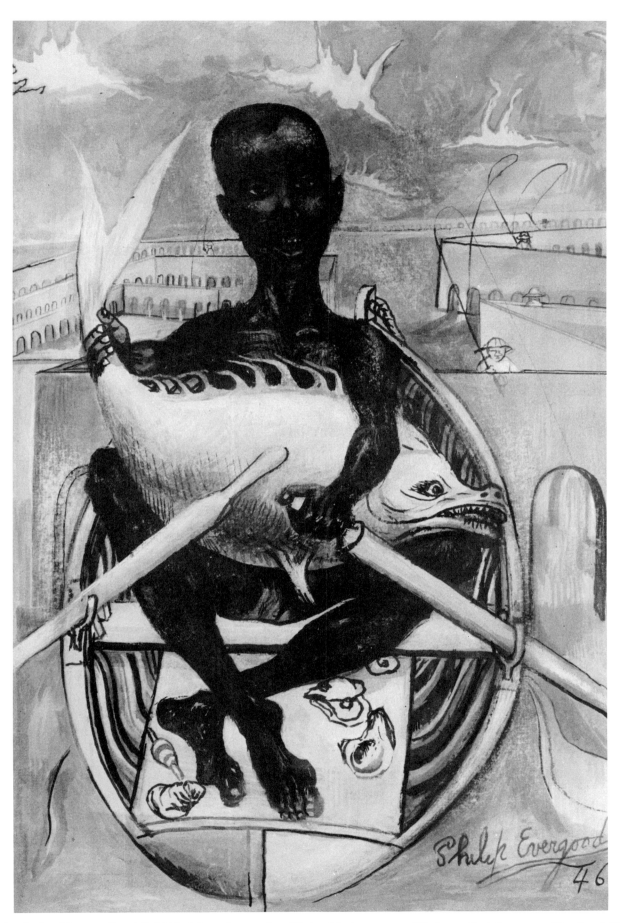

63. Study for "Dream Catch", 1946, ink and gouache, 15½ x 10¼, courtesy Wadsworth Atheneum, Hartford, Conn.

64. Mabel Dobkin, (1945), pen and ink with wash, 24⅛ x 18⅛, Mr. and Mrs. David Holtzmann, New York.

65. Seated Dancer, (c.1945), pen and orange ink, pencil, 17 x 13⅞, Alfredo Valente, New York. (Inscribed in 1949.)

66. Illustration for Gogol's "The Overcoat", (1951), brush and ink over watercolor,
    22 x 15, Mr. and Mrs. Morris Primoff, New York.

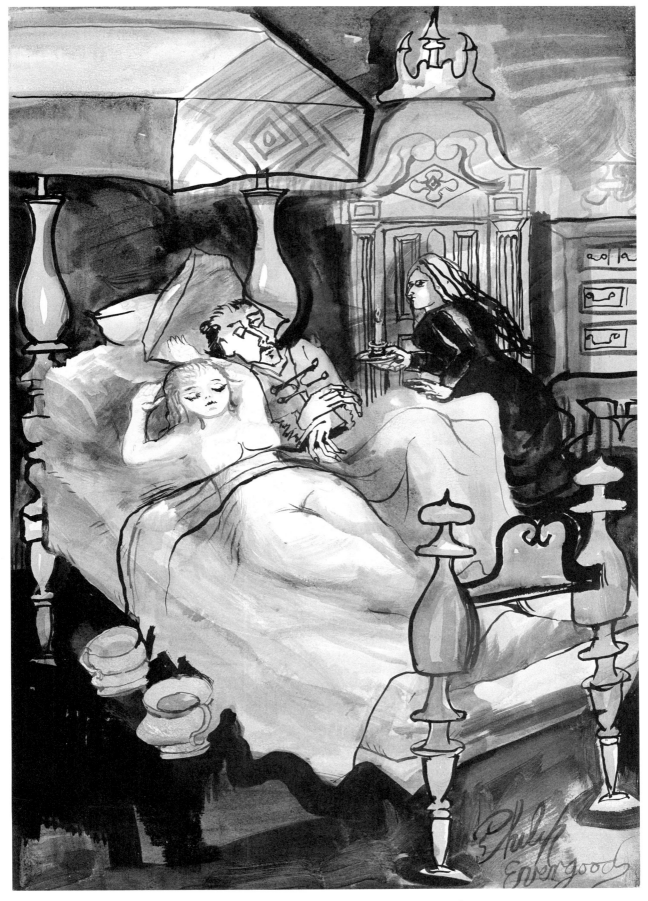

67. Illustration for Gogol's "The Coach", (1951), brush and ink over watercolor,
    22 x 15, Mr. and Mrs. Morris Primoff, New York.

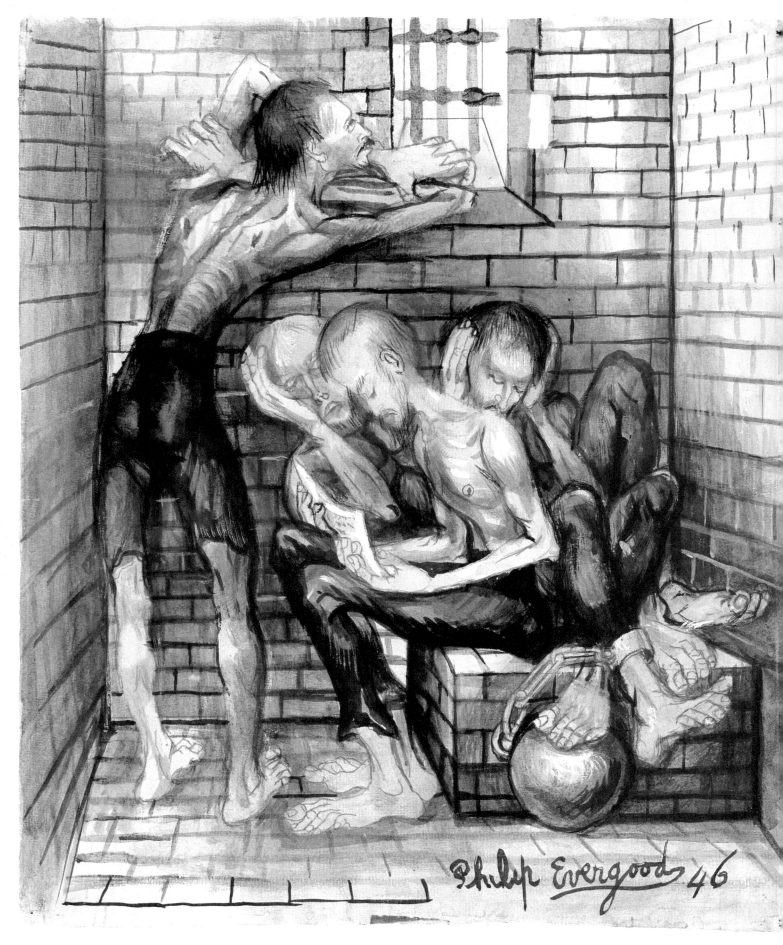

68. The Indestructibles, 1946, pencil and watercolor, 16⅞ x 14, Ida and Moses Soyer, New York.

69. Girl Reading, 1954, ink and charcoal, 33¼ x 25¼, Joseph H. Hirshhorn, New York.

71. Study for "Girl With Sunflowers", (1951), charcoal,
25½ x 19¼, Tirca Karlis Gallery, Provincetown, Mass.

70. Mordkin the Dancer, (c.1942), charcoal, 29½ x 19,
Herman Binder, Detroit.

72. Nude in a Chair, 1950, pencil, 22½ x 19, Julia Evergood, New York.

73. First Study for "The Jester", (1950), pen and ink, wash, 7 x 11, Sol Brody, Philadelphia.

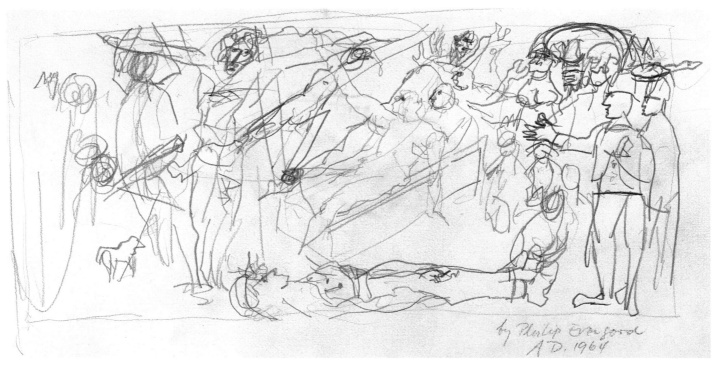

74. Study for "New Lazarus", (c.1954), pencil, 13 x 20, Alexander Dobkin, New York.

75. Outdoor Movie, Iowa, 1955, pencil, 17¾ x 11¾, the artist.

76. **Dead Christ, after Grünewald's Isenheim Altarpiece (predella), (1950), pencil, 12 x 17¾, the artist.**

77. Mary, Saint John and the Lamb of God, after Grünewald's Isenheim Altarpiece (The Crucifixion), (1950), pencil, 12 x 17¾, the artist.

from Grunewald
Philip Evergood

To Alex Dobkin who
rediscovered for me the beauty o
the power of Grunewald.

Philip Evergood

78. Christ Crucified, after Grünewald's Isenheim Altarpiece (The Crucifixion), (1950), pencil, 17¾ x 12, Alexander Dobkin, New York.

79. Men and Machines (Mesabi Mines), or, Mesabi's Big Dipper, (1955), pencil, 39¾ x 30⅛, Mark LaFarge, New York.

80. *Strange Birds*, (1954), ink and watercolor, 38 x 25, Joseph H. Hirshhorn, New York.

81. Mother and Child, 1957, pencil, 23⅞ x 18, Terry Dintenfass, New York.

82. Woman with the Hair (Julia), 1955, brush and ink, 36¾ x 23¼ sight, Mr. and Mrs. Sol Fishko, New York.

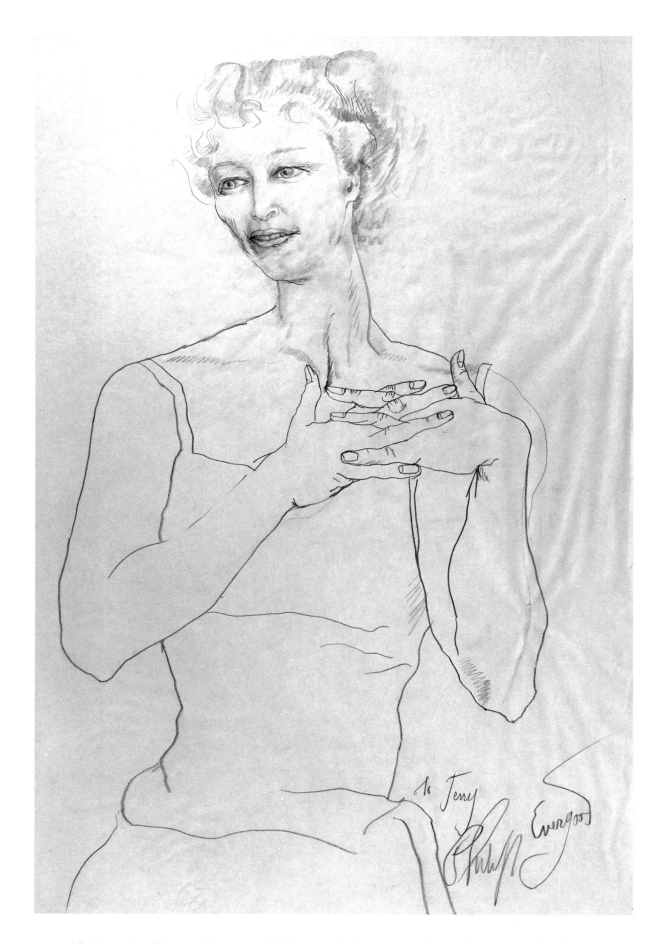

83. Portrait of Terry Dintenfass, (1959), pencil, 35½ x 24½, Terry Dintenfass, New York.

84. Pensive Nude, (c.1958), pen and ink, 24 x 18¾, Terry Dintenfass, New York.

85. Miss Barzansky in Summertime, 1961, ink and wash, 31 x 22⅞, Mrs. David Forer, New York.

86. Dancer, 1960, charcoal, 18¾ x 27¾, Mr. and Mrs. Boris M. Tarna, Tokyo.

87. Three Little Girls, 1961, pencil, 38¼ x 25½, Miss Katherine Gwathmey and Miss Ida Tarrington Gwathmey, New York.

88. Let Us Harvest the Earth Together, 1961, brush and ink, wash, 24⅝ x 19, Mark LaFarge, New York.

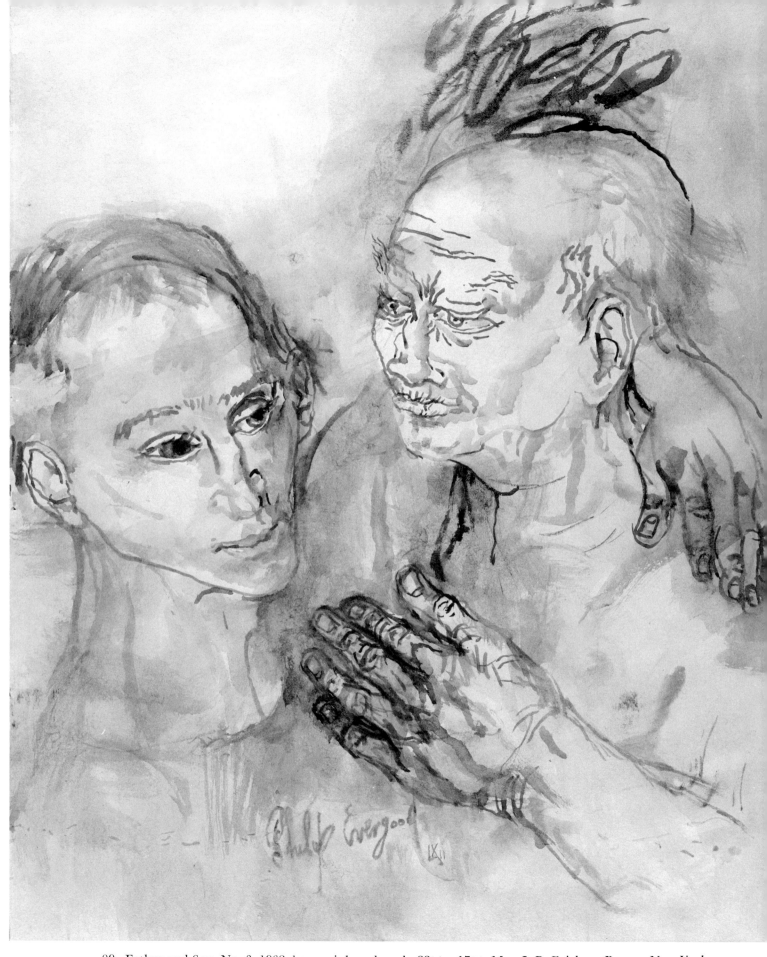

89. Father and Son, No. 3, 1962, brown ink and wash, 22½ x 17⅝, Mrs. J. P. Erichsen-Brown, New York.

90. Two Mothers, 1961, brush and brown ink, 38½ x 26½, Mr. and Mrs. Frederick R. Mebel, Rockville Centre, N.Y.

91. Suburban Twilight, 1960, charcoal and ink, 327/8 x 20, Andrew Dintenfass, New York.

92. Boy With Shovel, 1960, brush and ink, wash, 20¼ x 15⅛, Mr. and Mrs. Raphael Soyer, New York.

93. The Happy Truckman, 1961, brush and ink, watercolor, 16½ x 21½, William J. Poplack, Birmingham, Mich.

94. Mother Love, 1960, brush and ink, 16¾ x 14, Mrs. Louis Smith, New York.

95. Dancer, 1962, pen and ink, 19½ x 14½,
Giorgio Chiaron Casone, Rome.

96. Conversation, 1961, charcoal, 26¾ x 20¾,
Joseph H. Hirshhorn, New York.

98. Woman with Dozing Dog, (c.1961),
22¾ x 18, private collection, New York.

97. Old Woman, 1963, pen and ink, 19 x 13½
(sight), Miss Edith Nivel, New York.

99. Lilies of the Field, 1960, sepia ink and wash, 30⅞ x 22¾, Mr. and Mrs. Benjamin Bell, Long Island City, N.Y.

100. Woman and Dogs, February 1962, pencil, 24⅞ x 19⅛, Julia Evergood, New York.

101. Playing Ball, 1962, charcoal, ink and wash, Mr. and Mrs. Stanley Mossman, 27¼ x 20¼ (sight), Owings Mills, Md.

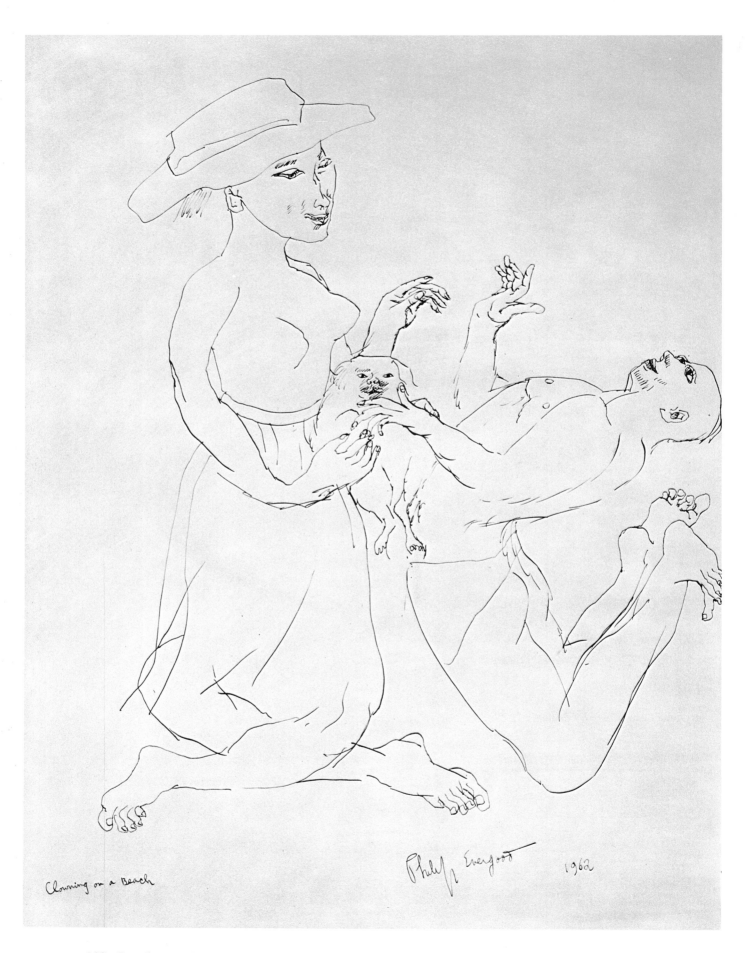

Clowning on a Beach

Philip Evergood 1962

102. Gwathmey Clowning on a Beach, 1962, pen and ink, 23 x 18¼, private collection, New York.

103. Girl in a Brocade Chemise, 1964, pencil, crayon, brush and ink, 24¼ x 19¼, Mr. and Mrs. Joseph J. Akston, New York.

104. Dance of the Fishbones, 1963, charcoal, watercolor, ink, 24⅜ x 19¼, Mr. and Mrs. Joseph J. Akston, New York.

105. Chairman of the Bored, 1963, colored inks and charcoal, 24¼ x 19¼, private collection, New York.

106. End of the Trail, 1962,
charcoal, sepia ink and wash,
18⅜ x 22⅝, private collection,
New York.

107. Study for "Abandoned Doll",
1962, charcoal and watercolor,
29 x 22⅞, private collection,
New York.

108. Charred Home and Old Sow with Her Litter, 1963, charcoal, inks, wash, 24⅝ x 19¼, private collection, New York.

FEMME A LA PIPE

109. Study for "Burden", (c.1963), charcoal and ink wash,
24⅝ x 19, Mr. and Mrs. Joel Turner, New York.

109a. Femme à la pipe, 1964, 30 x 20
Mr. and Mrs. Joseph J. Akston, New York.

110. **Young Man Home From Work**, 1962, ink, chalk, watercolor, 24½ x 19¼, Mr. and Mrs. Jay Topkis, New York.

111. Carpaccio and the Dudas, 1964, brush and ink, watercolor, 24¼ x 19⅛, Mr. and Mrs. Joseph J. Akston, New York.

112. Inheritance: The Blues, (1964), ink and wash, 29 x 23⅛, Moses Asch (Folkways Records), New York.
(Jacket for record album "Music Down Home", edited by Charles Edward Smith.)

113. Girl with the Giaconda Smile, 1965, pencil, 20⅜ x 15⅞, Mr. and Mrs. Joseph J. Akston, New York.

114. New Widow at the Mines, 1965, brush and ink, wash, 28⅞ x 23, Mr. and Mrs. Joseph J. Akston, New York.

Prints

NOTE: Most of Evergood's early prints were not published in set editions, and it is impossible at this point to determine the number of impressions pulled. In addition, certain of the etchings listed in *bibl. 44* no longer exist due either to loss or reworking of the plates, or to the disappearance of the few existing copies. Many of the early etchings have several alternate titles, further confusing the identification problem. The dates listed here in parentheses have been ascribed by the author in collaboration with the artist. Dimensions given are those of the plate or stone where these were at all definable; otherwise the sheets have been measured.   L.R.L.

115. Portrait of an Old Jew, 1924, drypoint, 6 x 5.

116. Portrait of the Artist as a Young Man
(Philip Reisman), 1924, etching, 5 x 3⅞.

117. Heaven, (1926), etching, 7⅞ x 9⅝.

118. Centaurs and Men, (1926-27), etching, 7 x 9¼.

119. Daughters of Cain, 1927, etching, 9¾ x 7¾.

120. Abraham, Isaac, and the Angel, 1927,
etching, 5 x 4.

121-126. ETCHINGS AND STUDIES
FOR MILTON'S *LYCIDAS*
(1928-29); see *bibl. 205*.

121. "Flames in the forehead of the
morning sky", 8 x 6¼.

122. "For we were nursed upon the selfsame hill", 7⅛ x 5¼.

123. [Study for no. 122], pencil, 8¼ x 11⅜, Hudson Walker, New York.

124. "The laureat hearse where Lycid lies", 5⅛ x 7¼.

125. "He asked the waves and asked the fellon winds", 6¼ x 8.

126. [Study for no. 125], pencil, 8¼ x 11⅜, Hudson Walker, New York.

127. Rhythm in Nature, (1928-29), etching, 3 x 4⅛.

128. Dryad, (1928-29), 3⅜ x 2½.

129. The Virgins, (1928-29), etching, 4 x 5.

130. Woodland Romance, (1928-29), etching,
4½ x 6½.

131. Alone With Nature, (1928-29), etching,
4⅜ x 6⅜.

132. The Bridge, (1928-29), etching, 4 x 5.

133. Woodland Reverie, (1928-29), etching, 6 x 8.

134. Poetry of Nature (Figures in the Park),
(1928-29), etching, 4½ x 6½.

135. The Ploughman Homeward Plods His
Weary Way, (1928-29), etching, 4 x 6.

136. Youth and a Phantom (The Phantom Horse), (1929-30), etching, 5 x 7.

137. The Sick Horse (1929-30), etching and engraving, 6¼ x 7½.

138. The Sick Horse (1928-29), pencil, 7¼ x 13⅜, the artist (drawn on the back of a menu from the Grand Ticino restaurant).

139. Suffering Woman, (1929-30), etching and engraving, 4½ x 6½.

140. Dance of the Virgins (Warrior's Cloak), (1929-30), etching and engraving, 4½ x 6⅜.

141. The Antique Urn, (1930), etching, engraving, drypoint, on brass plate, 11¾ x 11.

142. Primitive Dance (1930-31), etching and engraving, 9½ x 16¼.

143. Introduction to a Dance, (1930), etching, 8⅛ x 10⅝.

144. Beginning of a Dance (1930), etching and engraving, 9½ x 16¼.

145. Drawing on a Wall (1930), etching, engraving, drypoint, 4½ x 10.

146. Menacing Black Horse (1930-31), etching, engraving, drypoint, 6 x 15½.

147. Adam and Eve, (1930),
     drypoint and engraving,
     9¾ x 7.

148. Woman and Centaur, (1930-31), etching, engraving, drypoint, 10¼ x 10.

149. Death of Absalom, (1930-31), etching, engraving, drypoint, 8 x 13¾.

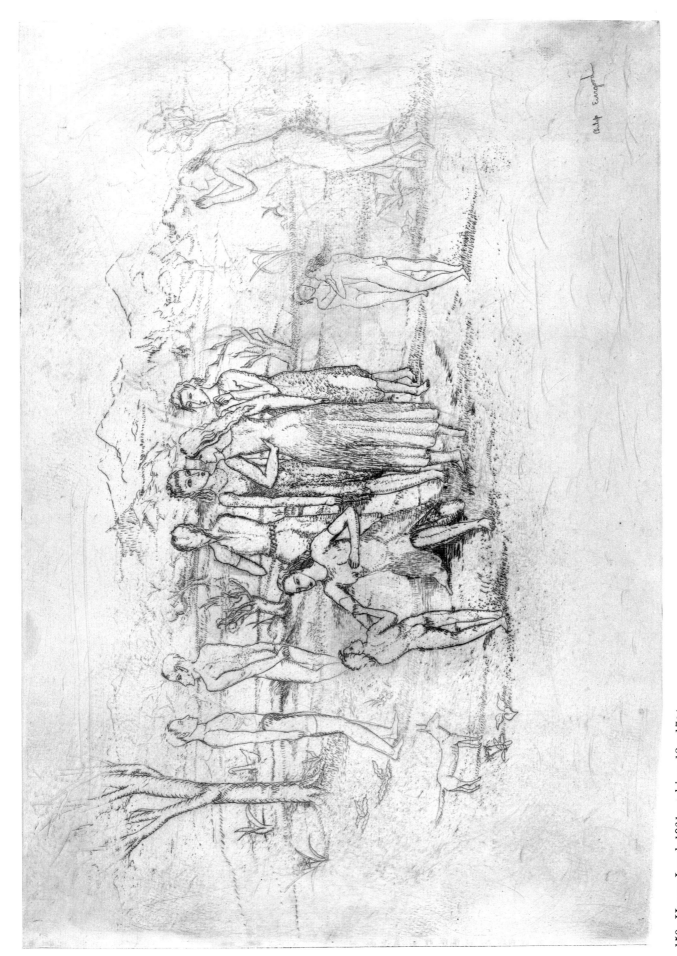

150. Happy Land, 1931, etching, 12 x 17¾.

151. The Encroaching City, (1938), etching, 7 x 12.

152. The Centaur is Gone (Footsteps in the Sand), (1936), etching, engraving,
   drypoint, on used photoengraving plate, 7⅛ x 4¾.

153. What Price Glory? (c.1936), lithograph, 8 x 11⅝.

154. Sorrowing Farmers, (1937), lithograph, 8½ x 12¼.

155. Aftermath of War, (1945),
etching and drypoint, 6⅞ x 9.

156. Still Life, (1944), lithograph, 11½ x 16¼. (Edition of 200 for ACA Gallery).

157. Portrait of a Miner, (1938), etching on steel, 7⅜ x 6½.
    (Special edition in color issued by ACA Gallery in connection with *bibl. 44.*)

158. City Lights I, (1940-41), lithograph (on zinc), 9½ x 12⅛.

159. City Lights II, (1940-41), lithograph (on zinc), 8⅜ x 11⅞. (Edition for the Kalamazoo Art Institute.)

160. City Landscape (Kalamazoo), (1940-41), etching, 5 x 7¾.

161. Kalamazoo Landscape, (1941-42), red and black chalk, 20 x 25⅝, Joseph H. Hirshhorn, New York.

162. Ice Cream Cones for Three, (c.1944), soft-ground and line etching, 12 x 9¾.

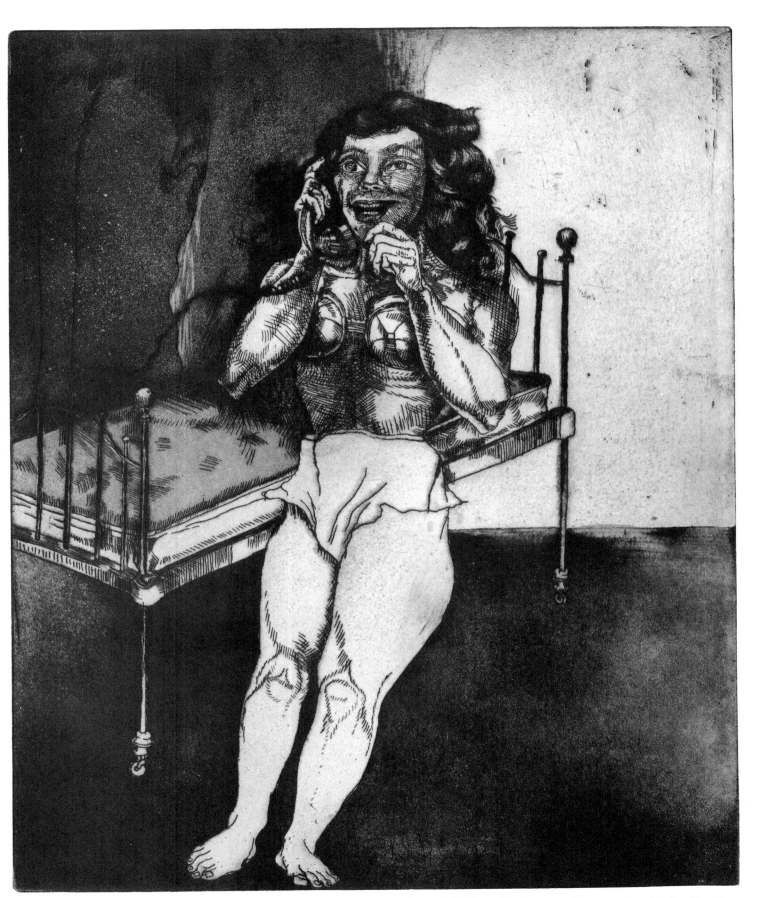

163. Mom, I'm Engaged, (c.1957), etching and aquatint, 16¾ x 13¾. (Collaboration between Evergood and John Page.)

Philip Evergood

Philip Evergood

Cool Doll in Pool

164. Cool Doll in Pool, 1960, lithograph (on zinc), 17½ x 12¼. (Edition of 200 for ACA Gallery.)

165. Success Team, 1960, lithograph (on zinc), 12⅜ x 18¾. (Edition of 200 for ACA Gallery.)

166. Self Portrait Without Hat (Sweet Self Portrait), 1961, lithograph (on zinc),
19 x 14⅞. (Edition of 50 for Terry Dintenfass Gallery.)

167. Self Portrait With Hat, 1961, lithograph (on zinc), 16⅜ x 15¼. (Edition of 50 for Terry Dintenfass Gallery.)

168. Me and My Dog, 1961, lithograph (on zinc), 17⅝ x 15⅞. (Edition of 50 for Terry Dintenfass Gallery.)

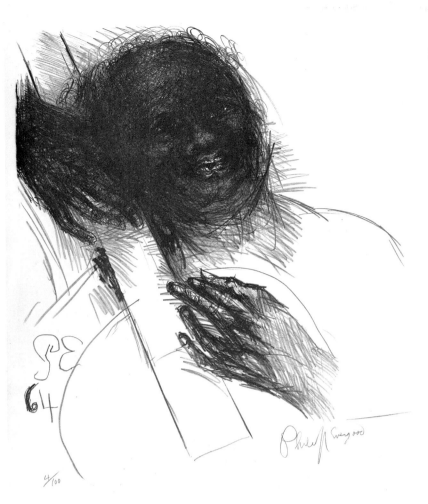

169. Joyous Song, 1964, lithograph (on zinc),
23½ x 19¼. (Edition of 100 for Gallery 63.)

170. Everybody's Christmas, 1964, lithograph
(on zinc), 23 x 17⅝.
(Edition of 100 for Gallery 63.)

172. Girl and Old Dog, 1965, lithograph (on zinc), 21 x 15⅛.

171. Harlequin and Columbine, 1964, lithograph (on zinc), 22¾ x 18⅛.

174. Woman in a Chekhov Mood, 1965, three-color lithograph (on zinc), 20½ x 17. (Edition of 100 for Sears and Roebuck, the Vincent Price Collection.)

173. Family, 1965, lithograph (on zinc) printed in black ink on blue, 21 x 15⅛.

Acknowledgments

My foremost debt is to the artist himself. With his wife, Julia Cross Evergood, he has given generously not only of his time and energy, but of his vigor and sensitivity as well. My deepest thanks are due to Mr. and Mrs. Joseph James Akston, who conceived this project and without whom it could not have been completed, and to Mr. Morris Primoff, whose aid has been of the utmost importance. Abe Lerner designed the book and, in addition, provided invaluable editorial assistance at every stage; Charles Edward Smith has given me the benefit of his perceptive memories of a long friendship with Evergood. I am grateful to Edith Nivel, Nina Larkin, Daniel Fogarty, and Doris Palca for their technical assistance, as well as to Elita Taylor, Cornelia Corson and Inga Forslund of the Museum of Modern Art Library, Edward Bryant of the Whitney Museum, Terry Dintenfass, and to Abram Lerner, Curator of the Joseph H. Hirshhorn Collection, who wrote the foreword, as well as to James A. Michener for his contribution. Finally, I must thank all of the collectors who graciously allowed me to examine their drawings and in many cases gave them up for several months so that reproductions could be made from the originals.   L. R. L.

175. Greek Vase, 1960, charcoal, 25¼ x 19, Mark LaFarge, New York.

Chronology

1901   October 26, Philip Howard Francis Dixon Blashki born to Flora Jane (Perry) and Myre Evergood Blashki in his father's studio on west 23rd Street, New York City. Mother born in England, father in Australia.

1905-08   Attended Ethical Culture School; took piano lessons from Mme. Rabagliatti and at age of six played in her Carnegie Hall concert; summers spent in New England; began to draw and paint.

1909   To England to be educated with financial support from his mother's family; attended various boarding schools, finally graduating from Stubbington House School in 1914.

1914   Took Royal Naval Training College examinations but after a five-month illness following appendicitis abandoned intentions of Navy career. Parents' name legally changed to Evergood, his father having become Miles some time earlier. Entered Eton College.

1915-19   War years spent at Eton; vacations in London with mother; father on active duty with Artists' Volunteer Unit, Army Medical Corps. Continued to do biblical and allegorical drawings.

1919   Graduated from Eton; to Brussels for tutoring in French, Latin, Mathematics. Passed entrance exams to Cambridge.

1919-21   At Cambridge University (Trinity Hall College). Left after decision to become an artist rather than to go into Law. To London where sculptor Havard Thomas introduced him to Henry Tonks, head of Department of Drawing and Painting at Slade School of Art (London University).

1921-23   Attended Slade School, receiving a Teacher's Certificate in Drawing after two years. 1922: Brief trip to Paris and then to U.S., where parents had settled.

1923   Returned to New York; studied drawing at the Art Students League under William von Schlegell and George Luks; night drawing classes at the Educational Alliance School.

1924-25   Learned etching technique from Philip Reisman. Left New York for canoe trip in Northern Europe with *National Geographic* writer, Melville Chater, with whom he parted company in Ostend after visiting The Hague, Ghent, Bruges, Antwerp, etc. Settled in Paris, with a studio in rue du Cherche-Midi.

Met Utrillo, Pascin, Signac, Bourdelle, Man Ray, Foujita and other artists. Short periods of study with Jean-Paul Laurens at Académie Julian and then with André Lhote. Worked independently, sharing models with Hiddingh and Siple. Met Julia Cross.

[151]

1924: Still life painting submitted to National Academy of Design, New York, by his mother, and exhibited there.

1925: etching (fig. 115) shown at Salon d'Automne. To Italy for several months—Milan, Venice, Florence, Naples and Rome (where he studied for about 6 weeks at British Academy); to Cagnes, on the French Riviera, staying in the home of Madame Rosalie, friend of Utrillo and Valadon.

1926   Returned to U.S. to be with his mother. Painted biblical scenes in a borrowed studio in Martinsville, N. J. Group of paintings shown at Dudensing Galleries.

1927   Death of mother from cancer. November: first one-man show, at Dudensing Galleries. Continued etching.

1928-30 Visits to Woodstock, N.Y. Joined Montross Gallery; 15 etchings included in one-man show there in 1929. (For further exhibitions, see bibliography, Sections III, V).

1930-31 Back to Paris, studio in rue Delambre; worked alone, earning living by carpentry, making stage-sets, boxing. Frequent visits to Stanley William Hayter's workshop where he learned engraving technique. Did many etchings, some printed by professionals, some by himself. Met Julia Cross again; they went to Spain, where he stayed six months, studying the Spanish Old Masters, El Greco in particular. To Paris for several months, then returned to U.S.

August 15, 1931: Married Julia Cross in New York City.

1931-34 Both Evergoods working at Gallery of American Indian Art. Lived in various downtown lofts and studios. Attended John Reed Club forums, exhibited work there. Increasing interest in music, especially jazz; through Charles Edward Smith, met Sidney Bechet, Leadbelly, Jazzbo Collins.

1932: First mural project, shown at Museum of Modern Art (bibl. 147).

1934-37 Joined Public Works of Art Project and later, its successor, the WPA. Briefly associated with Midtown Galleries. Did first lithographs (figs. 153, 154). Joined Artists Committee of Action; American Artists Congress; elected to An American Group. Founding member of Artists Union (president, 1937); member American Society of Painters, Sculptors and Gravers, mural section of Federal Art Project. Took part in "219 Strike" protesting treatment of artists by WPA.

1935: awarded M. V. Kohnstamm prize, Art Institute of Chicago; controversy followed (bibl. 152).

1934-37: Did mural in Richmond Hill Public Library, Long Island, which was protested and picketed by townspeople for its "gross corporeal references", and finally retained through active support of artists groups and the N.Y.C. Art Commission, headed by Ernest Peixotto (bibl. 42).

1936-37: Volunteer on faculty of American Artists School. Moved to Woodside, Long Island.

1937   Joined Herman Baron's ACA Gallery, where he remained until 1961. Participated in National Job March to Washington in support of unemployed workers. Controversy in Australia over purchase of Art on the Beach for the National Gallery of Victoria (bibl. 43).

1938   Death of father in Australia. Completed mural in U.S. Post Office, Jackson, Georgia, a government commission which also met local opposition; subject: Cotton from Field to Mill. Appointed full-time managing supervisor of Easel Division of New York WPA project (bibl. 40).

1939   Trips to Hoboken and Weehauken, with other artists, to expose bad conditions under Mayor Hague (see *fig. 10*). On jury, and included in exhibition at New York World's Fair.

1940-42 Resident artist at Kalamazoo College, Michigan, under Carnegie Corporation Grant. Summer 1941: in the East for vacation and hospitalized for serious intestinal obstruction; several operations, slow recovery from apparent cancer. Returned to complete mural, *The Bridge of Life,* at Kalamazoo College. Lithograph (*fig. 159*) commissioned by Kalamazoo Art Institute.

1942   Joined Artists League of America. Awarded sixth prize at the Artists for Victory exhibition, Metropolitan Museum of Art, New York (*bibl. 162*). Winter 1942-43: taught once a week at Muhlenberg College, Allentown, Pa. Private classes in Bethlehem, Pa. and at Settlement Music School, Philadelphia.

1943   February: Gave up these jobs to accept appointment by War Department to record pictorially the "impact of battle" with 19 other artists; tentatively assigned to the invasion of Africa; contracts signed, innoculations completed, etc., when he, Anton Refregier and William Gropper were rejected for having "joined the fight against Fascism too early". Worked at the Midtown Frame Shop; was able to go back to painting when the New York collector, Joseph Hirshhorn, bought several pictures.

1944   Joined Independent Voters Committee to work for Roosevelt's re-election. Awarded second prize in the Pepsi Cola "Portrait of America" competition (*bibl. 167*). Painted illustrations for a Russian American Friendship calendar (*bibl. 71*). Taught for a few months at State, County and Municipal Workers Union, CIO, with Frank Kleinholz.

1945   Left Woodside for newly bought house on Bank Street, Greenwich Village. To Houston, Texas, to illustrate article on cotton for *Fortune* magazine (*bibl. 207*). Awarded second honorable mention at the Carnegie Institute (*bibl. 157*).

1946   Retrospective exhibition at ACA accompanied by book with text by Oliver Larkin (*bibl. 44*), special color edition of etching (*fig. 157*). Taught at the Contemporary School of Art, Brooklyn, and at the Jefferson School, New York. Awarded second prize, Franklin D. Roosevelt Competition, ACA Gallery; William H. Tuthill Prize, Art Institute of Chicago; Alexander Shilling Purchase award (painting, *No Sale,* to Baltimore Museum of Art).

        Sold Bank Street house and moved to Patchogue at doctor's orders; end of very active social involvement period. Group of etching plates lost when printer moved during the year's confusion.

1947   Awarded second prize at La Tausca Art Competition, Riverside Museum (*bibl. 177*) for the painting *Dream Catch.*

1948   Included in Venice Biennale (*bibl. 182*).

1949   American Prize, Hallmark Art Award; Carol H. Beck Gold Medal for *Her World,* Pennsylvania Academy of Fine Arts; second prize Carnegie Institute, Pittsburgh, for *Leda in High Places* (*bibl. 157*).

1951   The film, *Philip Evergood* (*bibl. 47*), shown at film festivals in Mexico City, Lucerne, Boston, and New York. First Prize, Long Island Art Festival for *New York Suzanna;* Second W. A. Clark purchase prize, and silver medal Corcoran Gallery of Art American exhibition for *Sunny Side of the Street.* Given a testimonial dinner, March 16, under auspices of the Art Division, National Council of Arts, Sciences and Professions. Ford Foundation purchase award (*The Tooters,* to Brooklyn Museum).

1952   Awarded $5,000 First Prize, Terry Art Institute National Competition, Miami, Fla. (*bibl. 190*), for painting *Happy Entrance.* Bought a re-modeled barn and moved to Southbury, Conn.

1953   Lectured at Kansas State Teachers College, Pittsburg, Kansas *(bibl. 26)*.

1955   Won First Prize, Baltimore Museum of Art, *The Seaport* exhibition for *American Shrimp Girl*. Summer: instructor in painting, University of Minnesota, Duluth.

1956   Grant for painting, American Academy of Arts and Letters.

1957-58 Taught at Iowa State Teachers College, Cedar Falls. 1958: Joseph E. Temple Gold Medal, Pennsylvania Academy of Fine Arts, for *Threshold to Success*.

1959   Elected to the National Institute of Arts and Letters. Included in American National Exhibition in Moscow *(bibl. 200)*.

1960   Retrospective exhibition at the Whitney Museum of American Art, circulated in the United States, accompanied by a book by John I. H. Baur *(bibl. 31)*. Two lithographs edited by ACA Gallery *(figs. 164, 165)*.

1961   Death of Herman Baron; joined Terry Dintenfass Gallery. Drawing Prize at the Pennsylvania Academy of Fine Arts. Two portfolios of early drawings stolen.

1962   Three lithographs *(figs. 166-68)* edited by Dintenfass Gallery. August: moved to old farmhouse in Bridgewater, Conn. Gallery 63 Inc. became Evergood's representative.

1964   Drawing commissioned by Folkways Record Company for record jacket of an anthology of the Blues, "Down Home", edited by Charles Edward Smith *(fig. 112)*; July: lectured at the Michigan State University Fine Arts Festival, and on radio station WKAR, Lansing. Appeared on *Art Voices on the Air (bibl. 30a)*. Two lithographs edited by Gallery 63 *(figs. 169, 170)*.

1965   Hammer Galleries became Evergood's representative; first one-man exhibition there in spring, 1966. Received citation from *Who's Who in America* "in recognition of his outstanding contribution in the field of Art. Mr. Evergood, in the face of mercurial fashions, has strengthened his position as one of America's foremost artists."

176. Queen, (1910), brush and ink, 10 x 8,
Emil Arnold, New York.

Bibliography

Sections I, III, V and VI are listed chronologically, Sections II and IV alphabetically. A complete one-man exhibition list is incorporated into Section III. Newspaper coverage has not been included except in Section I.   L.R.L.

I. BY EVERGOOD (For additional statements see bibl. 31, 44, 53, 54, 72, 78, 80, 81, 87, 88, 91, 99, 110, 114, 132, 133, 157, 164, 183, 188, 194.)

1. "Question and Answer", *Art Front*, v.3, no.1, Feb. 1937, p.9-10.
2. "Building a New Art School", *Art Front*, v.3, no.3-4, Apr. 1937, p.21.
3. [On the Coffee-Pepper Bill] *In*, "Peyton Boswell Comments", *Art Digest*, v.12, no.11, Mar.1, 1938, p.3.
4. "Should the Nation Support its Art?" *Direction*, v.1, no.4, Apr. 1938, p.2-5.
5. "Foreword", *In, Gillen, Kallem, Neuwirth, Shulman*, ACA Gallery, New York, Sept. 1938.
6. "Should Art Prettify Heroes?" *Daily Worker*, Nov.2, 1942.
7. "Soviet Posters", *Daily Worker*, Sept.25, 1943.
8. "Sure, I'm a Social Painter", *Magazine of Art*, v.36, no.7, Nov. 1943, p.254-259.
9. "William Gropper", *New Masses*, v.50, no.9, Feb.29, 1944, p.26-27. (Also issued as "Bill Gropper", foreword, in ACA Gallery catalogue, Feb.7-27, 1944).
10. "Foreword", *In, Mexican Artist Conrado Vasquez*, ACA Gallery, New York, May 1944.
11. "My Vote—and Why: a Symposium on the Presidential Campaign", *New Masses*, v.53, no.2, Oct.10, 1944, p.9-10.
12. "Social Art: Its Background", *American Contemporary Art*, v.1, no.9, Nov. 1944, p.3-5; "Social Art Today", v.1, no.10, Dec. 1944, p.4-8. (Originally an address: "Fundamentals, Functions, Frameworks of Art: The Claims of Modernity and Humanity", given at Smith College, Northampton, Mass., 1944).
13. "David Burliuk", *Daily Worker*, Dec.22, 1944.
14. [Letter on the] "American Art Situation", *Daily Worker*, Jan.12, 1945.
15. "Social Surrealism?", *New Masses*, v.54, no.7, Feb.13, 1945, p.22. (Letter to the editor, in "Reader's Forum").
16. "Anton Refregier", *Daily Worker*, Mar.18, 1945.
17. "An Artist Observes the Critic", *American Contemporary Art*, v.2, no.3-4, May-June 1945, p.5-6. (Lecture given at dinner in honor of Elizabeth McCausland, May 28, 1945).
18. "About Artists by Artists: The Albrights", *New Masses*, v.57, no.9, Nov.27, 1945, p.15-16.

19. "The Miner: Eight Drawings by Philip Evergood", *Mainstream*, v.1, no.4, Fall 1947, p.453-460. (Introductory note by Harry Gottlieb, p.452).
20. [Harry Davis], *In, Harry Davis, Painter*, privately published, New York, 1949, p.6.
21. "Evergood in Defense of Evergood", *Art Digest*, v.24, no.7, Jan.1, 1950, p.3, 23. (Letter to the editor in reply to previous letter by G. Chigi: bibl. 157).
22. *The Artist and the Museum: A Conference Report*, American Artists Group, Inc., New York, 1951, p.51-53. (Report of the Third Woodstock Art Conference, Sept.1-2, 1950; Evergood participant in final session. Excerpt of Evergood speech published in *Newsletter* [Artists Equity Association], v.3, no.3, Oct.15, 1950, p.4-5.)
23. "A Juror's Statement", *The Corcoran Gallery of Art Bulletin*, v.5, no.1, Nov. 1951, p.3-4. (Concerning the 6th Annual Area Exhibition at the Corcoran Gallery).
24. "Statement", *Reality*, v.1, no.1, Spring 1953, p.1. (Joint statement signed by 46 artists; reprinted *Reality* no.3, Summer 1955, p.2.)
25. "Take Your Choice", *Reality*, v.1, no.2, Spring 1954, p.6.
26. "Art in Our Time", *The Educational Leader*, v.18, no.1, July 1, 1954, p.3-19. (Entire issue devoted to Evergood address, originally given at Kansas State Teachers College, Pittsburg, Kansas, Dec. 1953).
27. "Foreword", *In, Remo Faruggio*, John Heller Gallery, New York, Nov.29-Dec.17, 1955.
28. "Foreword", *In*, Willard, Charlotte, *Moses Soyer*, The World Publishing Company, Cleveland and New York, 1962, p.13-16.
29. "The Finished Product Should Be Invigorating" and "Realism or Representation Will Never be Outmoded", *In* Protter, Eric, ed., *Painters on Painting*, Universal Library, Grosset & Dunlap, New York, 1963, p.235-236.
30. "An Interview with Philip Evergood", *Art Voices*, v.2, no.10, Dec. 1963, p.8-9. (Interview by Gordon Brown; Evergood reproduction on cover).
30a. "Philip Evergood", *Art Voices on the Air*, Mar.12, 1964. (Radio interview with Gordon Brown; not the same as bibl. 30).

II. BOOKS AND ARTICLES ON EVERGOOD (See also Section III for one-man exhibition catalogues and brief reviews)

31. Baur, John I. H., *Philip Evergood*, Whitney Museum of American Art and Frederick A. Praeger, New York, 1960, 125p. (Includes chronology, catalogue of retrospective exhibition at Whitney and elsewhere, selected bibliography).
32. Blomshield, John, "Philip Evergood", *'47 the Magazine of the Year*, v.1, June 1947, p.140-145.
33. Burger, William Thor, "Evergood: Pioneering a New Art", *New Masses*, v.59, no.8, May 21, 1946, p.7-9.
34. Dennison, George, "Month in Review", *Arts*, v.34, no.8, May 1960 p.50-53. (Entire article on Evergood; reprinted in *Arts Yearbook* no.6, 1962, p.112-114).
35. Dunham, Alice, "The Courage of Philip Evergood", *Mainstream*, v.13, no.6, June 1960, p.56-60.
36. "Esquire's Art Institute III", *Esquire*, v.24, no.4, Oct. 1945, p.87.
37. "Ever Great Evergood", *Newsweek*, v.23, no.13, Mar. 27, 1944, p.93-94.
38. [Evergood], *Russky Golos*, Apr.25, 1948, p.13. (Text in Russian).
39. "Evergood Cops First Prize at Terry Exhibition", *Art Students League News*, v.5, no.3, Mar.15, 1952, p.4.
40. "Evergood Heads Easel Project", *Art Digest*, v.13, no.5, Dec.1, 1938, p.34.
41. "Evergood's Good and Bad", *Newsweek*, v.27, no.19, May 13, 1946, p.98.
42. "Evergood's Lusty Mural Stirs Citizen Wrath", *Art Digest*, v.12, no.17, June 1, 1938, p.18.
43. "First Modern American Canvas Starts Fight in Australia's National Gallery", *Life*, v.3, no.14, Oct.4, 1937, p.126.
44. Larkin, Oliver, "The Humanist Realism of Philip Evergood", *In, 20 Years of Evergood*, ACA Gallery and Simon and Schuster, New York, 1946, p.13-23. (Also includes statement by the artist, p.25-27; extensive documentation, p.30-108; catalogue of paintings, plates, works in public collections, catalogue of prints, murals and illustrations, one-man exhibitions, awards, chronology, and bibliography including list of newspaper reviews).
45. McCausland, Elizabeth, "The Plastic Organization of Philip Evergood", *Parnassus*, v.11, no.3, Mar. 1939, p.19-21.
46. "More in Sorrow", *Time*, v.75, no.16, Apr. 18, 1960, p.92-93.
47. *Philip Evergood*, nineteen-minute film, released April 15, 1953; directed and photographed by Howard Bird, score by William Ames, Brandon Films, New York.
48. Porter, Fairfield, "Evergood Paints a Picture", *Art News*, v.50, no.9, Jan. 1952, p.30-33, 55-56.
49. Rothe, Anna and Demarest, Helen, eds., "Philip Evergood", *In, Current Biography*, H. W. Wilson, New York, 1945, p.191-193.
50. Salpeter, Harry, "About Philip Evergood", *Coronet*, v.2, no.1, May 1937, p.174-175.
51. Smith, Charles Edward, "Evergood", unpublished typescript, 12p., 1961.
52. Solman, Joseph, "Philip Evergood", *Masses and Mainstream*, v.1, no.4, June 1948, p.90-93.
53. *"Time* for Evergood", *UMD Summer Calendar*, v.4, no.7, July 29, 1955, p.3. (From the University of Minnesota, Duluth Branch; includes quotations from the artist).
54. Tworkov, Jack, "Philip Evergood, Imaginative Realist: A Report of an Interview", *New York Artist*, v.1, no.2, Apr. 1940, p.3-4.
55. Valente, Alfredo, "Philip Evergood", *Peacock Alley*, v.6, no.11, May 1946, p.30.

III. ONE-MAN EXHIBITION CATALOGUES AND REVIEWS (Including complete chronological list of one-man exhibitions)

56. **Dudensing Galleries, New York, Nov. 1927.** Reviewed by Murdock Pemberton, *New Yorker*, v.3, no.40, Nov.19, 1927, p.96-97; Marya Mannes, *Creative Art*, v.1, no.3, Dec. 1927, p.xv.
57. **Montross Gallery, New York, Dec. 1929.** Reviewed in *Art News*, v.28, no.12, Dec.21, 1929, p.11.
58. **Balzac Galleries, New York, Dec. 1931.** Reviewed by Murdock Pemberton, *New Yorker*, v.7, no.45, Dec.26, 1931, p.48.
59. **Montross Gallery, New York, Mar.13-25, 1933.** 2p. catalogue. Reviewed in *Art News*, v.31, no.25, Mar.18, 1933, p.10; *Art Digest*, v.7, no.13, Apr.1, 1933, p. 16.
60. **Montross Gallery, New York, Jan.21-Feb.2, 1935.** 2p. catalogue. Reviewed in *Art Digest*, v.9, no.9, Feb.1, 1935, p.16.
61. **Hollins College, Virginia, 1935** (Drawings).
62. **Denver Art Museum, Denver, Colorado, 1936.**
63. **The Melbourne Atheneum, Melbourne, Australia, June 28-July 10, 1937.** (With Miles Evergood).
64. **ACA Gallery, New York, Feb.20-Mar.6, 1938.** 12p. catalogue, text by Herman Baron; held in connection with the Midtown Galleries. Reviewed by Jeannette Lowe, *Art News*, v.36, no.22, Feb.26, 1938, p.13; *Art Digest*, v.12; no.11, Mar.1, 1938; p.26; *Time*, v.31, no.10, Mar.7, 1938, p.39.
65. **ACA Gallery, New York, Mar.24-Apr.13, 1940.** 10p. catalogue, texts by William Gropper and Herman Baron. Reviewed by Edward Alden Jewell, *New York Times*, Mar. 27, 1940; Jeannette Lowe, *Art News*, v.38, no.26, Mar.30, 1940, p.17; Elizabeth McCausland, *Parnassus*, v.12, no.4, Apr. 1940, p.34, 36-37, il. p. 44; *Art Digest*, v.14, no.13, Apr.1, 1940, p.20.
66. **Kalamazoo Institute of Arts, Art Center, Kalamazoo, Michigan, Feb. 1941.**
67. **McDonald Gallery, New York, Apr. 1941 (Drawings).**
68. **ACA Gallery, New York, Oct.11-31, 1942.** 10p. catalogue, text by Sidney Lawrence. Reviewed in *Art News*, v.41, no.11, Oct.15, 1942, p.27, il. p.28; Robert M. Coates, *New Yorker*, v.18 no.36 Oct. 24, 1942, p.77; Manny Farber, *Magazine of Art*, v.35, no.7, Nov. 1942, p.261, 269; *Art Digest*, v.17, no.3, Nov.1, 1942, p.9.
69. **Lehigh University, Bethlehem, Pa., 1943 (?) (Drawings and Prints).**
70. **ACA Gallery, New York, Mar.13-Apr.1, 1944.** 14p.

catalogue, texts by John Davies Stamm and Moses Soyer. Reviewed by Aline B. Louchheim, *Art News*, v.43, no.3, Mar.15, 1944, p.16; Maude Riley, *Art Digest*, v.18, no.12, Mar.15, 1944, p.17.

71. **ACA Gallery, New York, Nov. 1944 ("The Story of Russian American Friendship", Paintings for calendar commissioned by Russian War Relief; also shown at the Worcester Art Museum and Baltimore Museum of Art).** Reviewed in *Pictures on Exhibit*, v.6, no.2, Nov. 1944, p.20-21; *Art News*, v.43, no.15, Nov.15, 1944, p.24; *Worcester Art Museum News Bulletin*, v.11, no.2, Nov. 1945, p.2; *Baltimore Museum of Art News*, v.8, no.6, Mar. 1946, p.2.

72. **ACA Gallery, New York, Apr.21-May 11, 1946.** Catalogue in book form, text by Oliver Larkin, see *bibl. 44*. Reviewed by Jo Gibbs, *Art Digest* v.20, no.14, Apr.15, 1946, p.9, 30; *Art News*, v.45, no.3, May 1946, p.35; *MKR's Art Outlook*, May 1946 (Includes statement by the artist; "An Artist's Faith"); *Time*, v.47, no.18, May6, 1946, p.64. *See also bibl. 33, 55*.

73. **ACA Gallery, New York, Apr.5-24, 1948.** 2p. catalogue. Reviewed by Renée Arb, *Art News*, v.47, no.2, Apr. 1948; p.32; Judith Kaye Reed, *Art Digest*, v.22, no.14, Apr.15, 1948, p.11.

74. **Norlyst Gallery, New York, Apr.9-24, 1948 ("Sprouts of Tender Years . . . Childhood Drawings").**

75. **ACA Gallery, New York, Feb.26-Mar.17, 1951.** 3p. catalogue, text by Herman Baron. Reviewed by Mary Cole, *Art Digest*, v.25, no.11, Mar.1, 1951, p.17; Henry McBride, *Art News*, v.50, no.2, Apr. 1951, p.49.

75a. **ACA Gallery, New York, 1951 (Illustrations for Gogol, see bibl. 201).**

76. **Garelick's Gallery, Detroit, Michigan, Jan.19-Feb.10, 1953.**

77. **Allen R. Hite Art Institute, University of Louisville, Louisville, Ky., Mar.9-28, 1953 (Drawings).** 4p. catalogue, text by Creighton Gilbert.

78. **ACA Gallery, New York, Mar.30-Apr.18, 1953.** 2p. catalogue, anonymous text including statement by the artist. Reviewed by Sam Feinstein, *Art Digest*, v.27, no.14, Apr.15, 1953, p.16; Larry Campbell, *Art News*, v.52, no.3, May 1953, p.45.

79. **Kansas State Teachers College, Pittsburg, Kansas, 1953.**

80. **Garelick's Gallery, Detroit, Michigan, Jan.24-Feb.5, 1955.** Catalogue includes statement by the artist.

81. **ACA Gallery, New York, Apr.11-30, 1955.** 2p. catalogue, text by Herman Baron, including artist's statement. Reviewed by Robert Coates, *New Yorker*, v.31, no.10, Apr.23, 1955, p.85; Lawrence Campbell, *Art News*, v.54, no.3, May 1955 p.46; Robert Rosenblum, *Art Digest*, v.29, no.15, May 1, 1955, p.24.

82. **Department of Art, Division of Humanities, University of Minnesota, Duluth, May 1-29, 1955.** 3p. catalogue with biography.

83. **Iowa State Teachers College, Cedar Falls, Iowa, 1957 (Drawings).**

84. **Newcomb Art School Galleries, Tulane University, New Orleans, La., Sept.24-Oct.5, 1957 (Drawings).**

85. **Whitney Museum of American Art, New York, Apr.6-May 22, 1960; also shown, 1960-61, Walker Art Center, Minneapolis, Minn., Wadsworth Atheneum, Hartford, Conn. (*see bibl. 87*), Des Moines Art Center, San Francisco Museum of Art, Colorado Springs Fine Arts Center, Munson-Williams-Proctor Institute, Utica, N.Y.** Catalogue in book form, text by John I.H. Baur, *see bibl. 31*. Reviewed by Dorothy Gees Seckler, *Art in America*, v.47, no.4, Winter 1959, p.100-105, 116, 123; Robert Coates, *New Yorker*, v.36, no.9, Apr.16, 1960, p. 143; Charles Michaelson, *RWSDU Record*, v.7, no.13, July 17, 1960, p.13. *See also bibl. 34, 46, 86.*

86. **ACA Gallery, New York, Apr.11-30, 1960.** 4p. catalogue, texts by Elizabeth McCausland and Herman Baron. Reviewed by Hubert Crehan, *Art News*, v.59, no.3, May 1960, p.40, 41, 63 (also review of Whitney exhibition).

87. **Wadsworth Atheneum, Hartford, Conn., Aug.3-Sept. 11, 1960 ("Doris Caesar—Philip Evergood").** Selection from Whitney Museum exhibition, *bibl. 85*, with separate catalogue. Text by Edward Bryant, p.18-24, biography p.18, 5 pl.

88. **ACA Gallery, New York, Apr.23-May 12, 1962.** 6p. catalogue, texts by John E. Brown, the artist, and Edward Bryant (excerpt from *bibl. 87*). Reviewed jointly with *bibl. 89* by Shelby Cooper, *Art News*, v.61, no.4, Summer 1962, p.46; Vivien Raynor, *Arts*, v.36, no.10, Sept. 1962, p.54.

89. **Terry Dintenfass Gallery, New York, April 23-May 19, 1962. (See *bibl. 88* for reviews.)**

90. **Ross-Talalay Gallery, New Haven, Conn., Oct.21-Nov.17, 1962 (in co-operation with Terry Dintenfass Gallery).**

91. **Galleria 63, Rome, Oct.19-Nov.7, 1963.** 10p. catalogue, texts by Renato Guttuso and the artist. Reviewed by Sigfrido Maovaz, *La Settimana a Roma*, v.14, no.42, Oct. 18-24, 1963, p.8; Duilio Morosini, *Paese Sera*, Oct.26, 1963; *Vita*, Oct.31, 1963, p.62-63; Dario Micacci, *L'Unità*, Nov.2, 1963.

92. **Gallery 63, New York, May 5-23, 1964.** 6p. catalogue, text by Edward Bryant. Reviewed by Gordon Brown, *Art Voices*, v.3, no.5, June 1964, p.9, il. p.1, of "Gallery Stroll"; Lawrence Campbell, *Art News*, v.63, no.4, Summer 1964, p.16.

92a. **Gallery 63, New York, Jan.19-30, 1965 (Drawings, with Umberto Romano).**

IV. GENERAL BOOKS AND ARTICLES INCLUDING EVERGOOD (See also Section V for group exhibition catalogues and reviews)

93. Abel, Walter, "The Law, the Maze and the Monster", *Magazine of Art*, v.41, no.1 Jan. 1948, p.6-11.

94. *America Today: A Book of 100 Prints*, American Artists Congress and Equinox Cooperative Press, New York, 1936, p.12, pl. 37.

95. "The Angry Art of the Thirties", *Fortune*, v.51, no.3, Mar. 1955, p.88-91.

96. Barr, Alfred H. Jr., *Painting and Sculpture in the Museum of Modern Art*, Museum of Modern Art and Simon and Schuster, New York, 1948, p.135, 146, 307.

97. Baur, John I.H., *Le Arti Figurative in America: 1900-1950*, Edizioni di Storia e Letteratura, Rome, 1954, p.36, 66, 69, 197, 198, pl. 41. (Translation by Giorgio Melchiori of *bibl. 100*).

98. Baur, John I.H., *Contemporary American Painting*, Book of the Month Club, New York, 1957, p.11-12, pl. 10. (Metropolitan Museum of Art Miniatures, Album xii).

99. Baur, John I.H., ed., *New Art in America: Fifty Painters of the 20th Century*, New York Graphic Society, Greenwich, Conn., 1957, p.113-117. (Statement by the

artist, p. 115).

100. Baur, John I.H., *Revolution and Tradition in Modern American Art*, Harvard University Press, Cambridge, Mass., 1951, p.20, 42, 44, 142, 143, fig.41. (Translation into Italian, bibl. 9₇.)

101. "Big Spender", *Time*, v.66, no.4, July 25, 1955, p.72-73.

102. Cahill, Holger and Barr, Alfred H. Jr., *Art in America in Modern Times*, Reynal & Hitchcock, New York, 1934, p.49. (New edition: *Art in America, A Complete Survey*, Halcyon House, New York, 1939, p.107).

103. Cahill, Holger, "Artists in War and Peace", *Studio*, v.130, no.628, July 1945, p.1-16.

104. Cahill, Holger, "In Our Time", *Magazine of Art*, v.39, no.7, Nov. 1946, p.308-325.

104a. Cahill, Holger, *New Horizons in American Art*, Museum of Modern Art, New York, 1936, p.139.

104b. Canaday, John, "On Innocence: With Reference to Philip Evergood", *In his Embattled Critic*, Noonday press, New York, 1962, p.158-162. (Originally printed in the *New York Times*, May 1, July 17, 1960.)

105. Carline, Richard, "Fine Art in Modern America", *Studio*, v.120, no.570, Sept. 1940, p.66-79.

106. Cerni, Vicente Aguilera, *Arte Norteamericano del siglo xx*, Fomento de Cultura, Valencia, 1957, p.111, pl. 87, 88.

107. Cheney Martha Candler, *Modern Art in America*, Whittlesey House, London, McGraw Hill, New York, 1939, p.129, 132, pl.80.

108. Cheney, Sheldon, *The Story of Modern Art*, Viking Press, New York, 1941, p.589, 591.

109. Chikadaiev, A., [article on American art in Soviet publication edited by Rockwell Kent], *Art of the USA*, Moscow, 1960. (Typescript in Library, Whitney Museum of American Art).

110. "Congress", *Time*, v.30, no.26, Dec.27, 1937, p.18. (Includes long quotation from Evergood address to the Second American Artists' Congress).

111. Crane, Aimée, ed., *Portrait of America*, Hyperion Press, New York, 1945, p.100.

112. Eliot, Alexander, *Three Hundred Years of American Painting*, Time, Inc., New York, 1957, p.237-239, 240.

113. Flanagan, George A., *Understand and Enjoy Modern Art*, Crowell, New York, 1962, p.311. (Revised edition of *How to Understand Modern Art, 1951*.)

114. Genauer, Emily, *Best of Art*, Doubleday & Co., Garden City, N.Y., 1948, p.74-76. (Includes statements by the artist).

115. Goodrich, Lloyd, and Baur, John I.H., *American Art of Our Century*, Whitney Museum of American Art and Frederick A. Praeger, New York, 1961, p.101-102, 103, 157-158, 163, 164, 189, 276.

116. Goodrich, Lloyd, *In,* "A Symposium: The State of American Art", *Magazine of Art*, v.42, no.3, Mar. 1949, p.90-91.

117. Grüber, L.F., "A Poster Campaign Against Infantile Paralysis", *Graphis*, no.29, 1950, p.56-61.

118. Gruskin, Alan D., *Painting in the U.S.A.*, Doubleday & Co., Garden City, N.Y., 1946, p.99.

119. Haftmann, Werner, *Painting in the Twentieth Century*, Frederick A. Praeger, New York, 1960, v.1, p.299, 387. (Revision of German editions published by Prestel, Munich, 1954-55 and 1957).

120. Hess, Thomas B., "Big Business Taste: The Johnson Collection", *Art News*, v.61, no.6, Oct. 1962, p.32-33, 55-56.

121. Kootz, Samuel M., *New Frontiers in American Painting*, Hastings House, New York, 1943, p.43, 44, 65, pl.30.

122. Larkin, Oliver W., *Art and Life in America*, Holt, Rinehart & Winston, New York, 1960, p.408, 424, 425, 430, 437-39, 441, 461, 480. (Revised and enlarged from original 1949 edition).

123. Lerman, Louis, *Winter Soldiers: The Story of a Conspiracy Against the Schools*, Committee for Defense of Public Education, New York, 1941.

124. McCurdy, Charles, ed., *Modern Art: A Pictorial Anthology*, MacMillan, New York, 1958, p.143, 146, 170, 182.

125. Mendelowitz, Daniel M., *A History of American Art*, Holt, Rinehart & Winston, 1960, p.578-579.

126. Moskowitz, Ira, ed., *Great Drawings of All Time*, Shorewood Publishers Inc., New York, 1962, v.4, pl.1099.

127. *Murals for the Community*, Federal Art Project, Works Progress Administration, New York, 1939, p.20. (mimeographed booklet).

128. Museum of Modern Art, *Art in Progress*, New York, 1944, p.65, 220.

129. Myers, Bernard S., ed., *Encyclopedia of Painting*, Crown, New York, 1955, p.171.

130. Myers, Bernard S., *Modern Art in the Making*, Whittlesey House, McGraw Hill Book Co., New York, Toronto, London, 1950, p.398-399, 402, fig.207.

131. National Gallery of Victoria, *Catalogue of the Collection, Melbourne*, 1948, p.45.

132. Nordness, Lee, ed., *Art USA Now*, Viking Press, New York, 1963, v.1, p.16, 106-109 plus 2p. text by Samuel Beizer. (Includes statement by the artist; general text by Allen S. Weller).

133. Pagano, Grace, *Contemporary American Painting: The Encyclopedia Britannica Collection*, Duell, Sloan & Pearce, New York, 1945, pl.39. (Includes statement by the artist).

134. Pierson, William H. Jr. and Davidson, Martha, eds., *Arts of the United States Today*, McGraw Hill, New York, 1960, p.78, 80, 81, 339-340.

135. Pousette-Dart, Nathaniel, ed., *American Painting Today*, Hastings House, New York, 1956 p.113.

136. Read, Helen Appleton, ed., *Pintura Contemporanea Norteamericana, New York,* 1941, p.47. (Book published in connection with traveling exhibitions in Latin America, May-Dec. 1941, organized by five New York museums and El Comite de arte de la oficina del coordinador de las relaciones culturales y commerciales entre las republicas americanas).

137. Richardson, H.P., *Painting in America: The Story of 450 Years*, Crowell, New York, 1956, p.405.

138. Richardson, E.P., *A Short History of Painting in America*, Crowell, New York, 1963, p.301, 307. (Abridgement of *bibl. 137* with new concluding chapter).

139. Sloan, John, *The Gist of Art*, American Artists Group, New York, 1939, p.42.

140. Soby, James Thrall, *Romantic Painting in America*, Museum of Modern Art, New York, 1943, p.42-43, 107, 134. (Published in connection with exhibition held Nov. 17, 1943-Feb.6, 1944).

141. "Speaking of Pictures: Artists Number Themselves Among Their Favorite Models", *Life*, v.15, no.17, Oct.25, 1943, p.12-14.

141a. Stephan, John, "Concerning Social Realism, Revivals and Ghosts", *It Is*, no.4, Autumn 1959, p.49-50.

142. Watson, Forbes, *American Painting Today*, American Federation of Arts, Washington, D.C., 1939, p.112.

143. *Who's Who in America*, Marquis—Who's Who, Chicago, 1962-63, v.32, p.950.

V. SELECTED GROUP EXHIBITIONS AND REVIEWS (Annuals and biennials are listed under the first year of Evergood's participation; group reviews are cited only when of particular interest in regard to Evergood. See also *bibl. 136, 140.*)

144. Pemberton, Murdock, "The Art Galleries", *New Yorker*, v.2, Sept.25, 1926, p.61-62. (Review of group of Evergood works at Dudensing Galleries).
145. *Contemporary American Paintings*, Corcoran Gallery of Art, Washington, D.C., 1928, 1939, 1949, 1951 (Reviewed in *Art Digest*, v.25, no.14, Apr.15, 1951, p.9-10; Thomas B. Hess, *Art News*, v.50, no.3, May 1951, p.42), 1953, 1957, 1959, 1961, 1963.
146. Pemberton, Murdock, "The Art Galleries", *New Yorker*, v.4, no.47, Jan.12, 1929, p.67. (Review of group show at Dudensing).
147. *Murals by American Painters and Photographers*, Museum of Modern Art, New York, May 3-31, 1932, p.23. (Texts by Lincoln Kirstein and Julien Levy).
148. *First Municipal Art Exhibition*, RCA building, The Forum, New York, Feb.28-Mar.31, 1934; also *Second Municipal Art Exhibition*, American Fine Arts Society Galleries, June 16-July 1, 1937.
149. *New York No-Jury Exhibition*, Salons of America Inc., RCA Building, New York, Apr.9-May 6, 1934.
150. *Annual Exhibition of the Pennsylvania Academy of Fine Arts, Philadelphia*, 1934, 1936, yearly, 1938-1954, 1956, 1958, 1962.
151. *American Genre*, Whitney Museum of American Art, New York, Mar.26-Apr.29, 1935. (Introduction by Lloyd Goodrich).
152. *Annual Exhibition of American Art*, Art Institute of Chicago, 1935, (Reviewed in *Art Digest*, v.10, no.3, Nov.1, 1935 p.5-6), 1937-38, 1940-41, 1941-42, 1942, 1943, 1944, 1945-46, 1947-48, 1951, 1954.
153. *Annual Exhibition*, Whitney Museum of American Art, New York, yearly since 1935.
154. *Annual Exhibition*, American Artists Congress, New York, 1937, 1938, 1939.
155. *50 American Prints: 1933-1938*, American Institute of Graphic Arts, New York, April-May, 1938. (Catalogue printed in *PM*, v.4, no.6, 1938, pl.2).
156. *1938 (Dedicated to the New Deal)*, ACA Gallery, New York, 1938. (Introduction by Herman Baron).
157. *[American and International] Exhibition of Paintings*, Carnegie Institute, Pittsburgh, 1938, 1939, 1940, 1943, 1944, 1945 (Reviewed by Jo Gibbs, *Art Digest*, v.20, no.2, Oct.15, 1945, p.5-6, 19; Edgar Kaufman Jr., *Art News*, v.44, no.13, Oct.15, 1945, p.11-13; *Time*, v.46, no.17, Oct. 22, 1945, p.77; John O'Connor Jr., *Carnegie Magazine*, v.19, no.5, Nov. 1945, p.139-146; (Includes statement by the artist), 1946, 1947, 1949 (Reviewed by Margaret Breuning, *Art Digest*, v.24, no.2, Oct.15,1949, p.7-9; *Time*, v.54, no. 17, Oct.24, 1949, p.71-72; Homer Saint-Gaudens, *Carnegie Magazine*, v.23, no.4, Nov. 1949, p.114-120; *Art Digest*, v.24, no.4, Nov.15, 1949, p.3: letter to the editor by G. Chigi), 1950, 1955.
157a. *An Exhibition of 100 Prints and Drawings from the Collection of James H. Lockhart, Jr.*, Carnegie Institute, Pittsburgh, May 4-June 30, 1939, p.210-211. (Introduction and notes by Robert McDonald).
158. *American Art Today*, New York World's Fair, National Art Society, 1939, p.28, 70. Reviewed by Elizabeth McCausland, *Parnassus*, v.11, no.5, May 1939, p.16-25.
159. Watson, Forbes, "Paintings by Artists under Forty", *Magazine of Art*, v.34, no.10, Dec. 1941, p.528-531, 542-543. (Review of Whitney exhibition by that title).

160. *A Decade of American Painting: 1930-1940*, Worcester Art Museum, Feb.18-Mar.22, 1942, p.14.
161. *Victory and Independence Exhibition*, Society of Independent Artists, New York, Apr. 1942.
162. *Artists for Victory*, Metropolitan Museum of Art, New York, Dec. 1942-Feb.22, 1943, p.4, 38; *Picture Book of the Prize Winners*, p.25. Reviewed by Alfred Frankfurter, *Art News*, v.41, no.16, Jan.1, 1942, p.8-13, 34.
163. *Exhibition of Distinguished Artists* [associated with the Art Students League], New York, Feb.7-28, 1943, p.56.
164. *Meet the Artist*, M.H. de Young Memorial Museum, San Francisco, 1943, p.51-52 (Includes extensive statement by the artist).
165. *Annual and Biennial Purchase Exhibitions*, Walker Art Center, Minneapolis, 1943, 1944, 1946, 1948, 1950.
166. *One Hundred Artists and Walkowitz*, Brooklyn Museum, Feb.9-Mar.12, 1944, p.12.
167. *Portrait of America*, Pepsi Cola annual exhibition, Metropolitan Museum of Art, New York, 1944. Reviewed in *Newsweek*, v.24, no.5, July 31, 1944, p.62; *Art News*, v.43, no.10, Aug.1, 1944, p.14-15, 27.
168. *Contemporary American Paintings*, Virginia Museum of Fine Arts, Richmond, 1944, 1946, 1948, 1954.
169. *Museum's Choice: Paintings by Contemporary Americans*, Art Gallery of Toronto, Feb. 1945.
170. *Contemporary American Paintings*, Worcester Art Museum, Feb.22-Mar.18, 1945.
171. *Contemporary American Painting, 1945*, California Palace of the Legion of Honor, San Francisco, May 17-June 17, 1945. (Introduction by Jermayne MacAgy).
172. *Summer Exhibition of Contemporary Art*, State University of Iowa, Iowa City, 1945, 1946, 1947, 1948.
173. *Paintings of the Year*, Pepsi-Cola Company's Third Annual Exhibition, National Academy of Design, New York, Oct.1-31, 1946.
174. *60 Americans since 1800*, Grand Central Art Galleries, New York, Nov.19-Dec.5, 1946.
175. *American Painting from the Eighteenth Century to the Present Day*, Tate Gallery, London, 1946 (Organized by the National Gallery, Washington, D.C.; Introduction by John Rothenstein).
176. Morse, John D., "Americans Abroad", *Magazine of Art*, v.40, no.1, Jan. 1947, p.21-25 (concerning IBM traveling exhibition: "American Industry Sponsors Art").
177. *Second Annual Exhibition of the La Tausca Collection*, Riverside Museum, New York, Jan. 1947. Reviewed by Jo Gibbs, *Art Digest*, v.21, no.9, Feb.1, 1947, p.12.
178. *One Hundred Years of American Painting*, Centennial Art Gallery, Utah State Fair Grounds, Salt Lake City, June 1-July 29, 1947, p.19.
179. *American Printmaking: 1913-1947*, Brooklyn Museum, Nov.18-Dec.16, 1947, p.20, 38. (Introduction by Jean Charlot; catalogue reprinted in *Print*, v.5, no.4, 1948, p.53, 55.)
180. *Advancing American Art*, U.S. State Department and War Assets Administration [1947?], pl.16. (Introduction by Hugo Weissgall).
181. *Catalogue of 117 Oil and Watercolor Originals by Leading American Artists Offered for Sale at Sealed Bid by War Assets Administration*, New York, June 1948, p.6.
182. *XXIV Biennale di Venezia*, 1948, p.304.
183. *Exhibition of Contemporary American Painting*,

University of Illinois, Urbana, 1948, 1949, 1950, 1951, 1953, 1955, 1957, 1961 (Catalogues include statements by the artist).
184. *The Hallmark Art Award*, Wildenstein, New York, 1949, p.19, 47. (Exhibition also circulated to museums in Boston, Washington, Los Angeles, Kansas City).
185. *American Painting Today*, Metropolitan Museum of Art, New York, 1950.
185a. *Evergood, Goodelman, Solman, Soyer*, ACA Gallery, New York, Mar.13-25, 1950.
186. *Diamond Jubilee Exhibition of Fine Art*, Art Students League, held at National Academy of Design, New York, Oct.8-29, 1950.
187. *American Painters of the Twentieth Century Represented in the Collections of the Metropolitan Museum of Art*, New York, 1950, pl.79. (Introduction by Robert Beverly Hale).
188. *Forty American Painters, 1940-1950*, University Gallery, University of Minnesota, Minneapolis, June 4-Aug. 30, 1951, p.20-23. (Introduction by H.H. Arnason; includes statement by the artist).
189. *Revolution and Tradition*, Brooklyn Museum, Nov. 15, 1951-Jan.6, 1952. (Based on *bibl. 100*).
190. Millier, Arthur, "Terry's Big-Scale Business: A Bonanza in Miami", *Art Digest*, v.26, no.11, Mar.1, 1952, p.10. (Review of the Terry Exhibition).
191. *75 Years of American Painting*, Marquette University, Milwaukee, Wis., Apr.22-May 3, 1956.
192. *13 Painters: 40 Years*, Mead Art Building, Amherst College, Amherst, Mass., May 2-27, 1956. (May 2, 1956, opening lecture by Evergood: "The Role of the Creative Artist in Society").
193. *Golden Years of American Drawings: 1905-1956*, Brooklyn Museum, Jan.22-Mar.17, 1957, p.19. (Text by Una Johnson).

194. *Fifty Contemporary American Artists*, Greenwich Gallery, New York, May 1-31, 1957, p.36-37 (Text by A.L. Chanin; statement by the artist).
195. *Art U.S.A.: 58*, Madison Square Garden, New York, Jan.17-26, 1958.
196. *The Museum and Its Friends*, Whitney Museum of American Art, New York, Apr.30-June 15, 1958.
197. *Nine American Artists*, Tweed Gallery, University of Minnesota, Duluth, Oct.19-Nov.23, 1958, p.19-22. (Preface by Orazio Fumagalli).
198. *Art U.S.A.: 59*, New York Coliseum, Apr.3-19, 1959, p.25.
199. *The Collection of the Sara Roby Foundation*, Whitney Museum of American Art, New York, Apr.29-June 14, 1959, p.9, 22.
200. *American Painting and Sculpture: American National Exhibition in Moscow*, Sokolniki Park, July 25-Sept.5, 1959 (Mimeographed translation of catalogue printed by Archives of American Art, Detroit; Selections from Exhibition shown at the Whitney Museum of American Art, New York, Oct.28-Nov.15, 1959.)
201. *Ten Modern Masters of American Art: 30 Works Selected from the Joseph H. Hirshhorn Collection*, circulated in the U.S.A., Jan. 1959-Jan. 1960, p.6, 16-17. (Introduction by John I.H. Baur).
202. [Members of the American Academy of Arts and Letters], Academy Galleries, New York, May 20-June 14, 1959.
203. *31 American Contemporary Artists*, ACA Gallery, New York, June 15-Aug.31, 1960, p.27-28. (Introduction, "The ACA Gallery: Impressions and Recollections" by Herman Baron, p.3-9).
204. *The Theatre Collects American Art*, Whitney Museum of American Art, New York, Apr.10-May 16, 1961. (Foreword by Eloise Spaeth).

VI. SELECTED BOOKS AND MAGAZINES ILLUSTRATED BY EVERGOOD
(See also bibl. 19, 123.)

205. Milton, John, *Lycidas*, Harry Lorin Binsse, New York, 1929. (Limited edition, 88 copies; includes 4 original etchings by Evergood).

206. *The Story of Russian American Friendship*, Russian War Relief, New York, 1944. (12 color plates published as 1945 calendar; see *bibl. 71*).

207. "Will Clayton's Cotton: I", *Fortune*, v.32, no.5, Nov. 1945, p.138-147; II, no.6, Dec. 1945, p. 158. (Illustrated by drawings and color plates).

208. [Political Cartoon], *New Masses*, v.58, no.8, Feb.19, 1946, p.4.
209. "Australia", *Fortune*, v.33, no.3, Mar. 1946. (Color advertisement for Container Can Corporation of America; also printed in other magazines).
209a. Osborne, Maybelle, "Mrs. Kochenski and the Problem Child", *Seventeen*, Feb. 1949.
210. Gogol, Nikolai, *Old Russian Stories*, Story Classics, Rodale Press, Emmaus, Pa., 1951. (Illustrated by gouaches and drawings).

177. Hitler Trying to Lay an Egg, (c.1942), pen and ink over pencil, 14 x 17, the artist.